Liberation, Love, and Creative Awakening: A Holistic Journey

David J Miller

Liberation, Love, and Creative Awakening: A Holistic Journey

Sacred Breeze Ministries

Sautee Nacoochee, Georgia, USA.

www.sacredbreeze.org

First Edition

ISBN: 979-8-9909446-1-9

DEDICATION

To my beloved first born son, Daniel Emerson Miller

CONTENTS

ACKNOWLEDGMENTS

I am grateful to my wife Stacey and to my children Daniel, Erin, Benjamin, and Jonathan for their love and support throughout this journey we call life.

I am grateful for the content and copy editorial support of my friends Bruce Alderman, Rev. Dr. Bruce Irwin, Chuck Anderson, and Chynna Mai.

PREFACE

Liberation, Love, and Creative Awakening provides instruction, exercises, and guided meditations to help release challenges, and to develop holistic understanding of consciousness, sacred energies, spirituality, and relationships. The text draws inspiration from psychology, physical and biological sciences, Buddhism, and theistic Judeo-Christian-Islamic texts. The goal is to help a person cultivate and share creative gifts for the benefit of self and others.

You, my friend, are precious. You are sacred beyond words. And you are beloved beyond words. More than that, you are important. You were crafted in a unique and wonderful way, with creative gifts meant to benefit yourself and others. And this is true no matter what your age, experience, or place in life.

Creative gifts, like people, come in all shapes and sizes. Some gifts are social, in nurturing, healing, and bringing comfort. Some are artistic and inspiring. Some gifts are practical, in building, maintaining, and organizing. And some gifts are inquisitive, in asking, learning, and sharing what is learned.

We are all, individually, and collectively, on a sacred journey. Our destination is the fulfillment of creative potential for the benefit of self and others. And the rewards encountered along the way include love, joy, accomplishment, healing, and reconciliation, in this life and beyond.

Imagine a world where every precious, creative being were to develop their unique gifts for the benefit of themselves and the universe. Human potential would be limitless! The challenges of conflict, disease, and suffering would be met with compassion and purpose, every human being would be celebrated, and everyone would reach their own creative and productive potential!

But, alas, challenges exist that prevent this hopeful vision from being fulfilled. You have challenges, I have challenges, and society has challenges. Everyone has challenges that hold us back, that limit, and that discourage.

The good news is that challenges also provide motivation to keep moving, keep learning, and keep sharing. Challenges also provide connection with others. Challenges shape us, and our gifts, to meet our own needs and the needs of others like us.

So, how does one get through the challenges and start reaping rewards? Chances are, you already have the tools you need, and you already share and reap some rewards. But sometimes the challenges feel overwhelming. What can make the journey easier, and more joyous?

The answer lies in knowledge of self and of others. And not just intellectual knowledge; deep understanding of thoughts, emotions, motivations, and spirituality. Understanding how consciousness works, and how sacred energies flow that contribute to physical, emotional, and spiritual health. And knowledge of how to form and nurture lasting, loving, authentic relationships.

You journey starts with acknowledging sacred self-worth and releasing challenges that prevent forward movement. Along the way, instructions and exercises cultivate understanding of consciousness, sacred energies, spirituality, and relationships. Guided meditations cultivate deep and compassionate connections within self, with Authentic Spirit, and with others. Within this physical existence and beyond.

No matter where you are in life, young or mature, male, female, or unique in gender and sexuality, spiritual, religious, or otherwise, healthy and fit, or burdened with physical, emotional, or spiritual challenges, knowledge and understanding can only make life better. Understanding opens doors, brings relief, healing, and hope that transcends experience.

So welcome to your Holistic Journey. Every journey takes place one step, one day at a time. And you are not alone! Authentic Spirit, Sacred Core Self, and others are here to encourage and guide you along the way. Your journey begins here and now.

I CREATIVE AFFIRMATION

Liberation, Love, and Creative Awakening explores the mysteries of consciousness, Spirituality, Sacred Energies in harmony with Neurochemistry, and the dynamics of healthy and loving relationships. The text draws inspiration from psychology, physical and biological science, Buddhism, and theistic Judeo-Christian-Islamic texts.

Each chapter offers instruction, exercises, and guided meditations developed to increase mindful self-awareness, release challenges that block creative engagement, cultivate creative energies, strengthen faith relationships within self and with Higher Power, cultivate compassion for self and others, and cultivating healthy and loving relationships.

People who benefit from this program include anyone interested in cultivating creativity while exploring consciousness, Spirituality, healthy relationships, and the nature of human existence. Others who may benefit include anyone seeking help with addiction, emotional, and relationship issues.

The meditation exercises in this program utilize breathing to stabilize thoughts and feelings. As a person progresses through the program and gains experience, deeper and more productive meditation levels are reached. People who have tried meditation in the past and find it is "not for them" may find this LLCA method easier to engage in than other approaches.

Some people are simply not comfortable with inward focused "sitting" meditation. While the meditation practice sections in each chapter help a person to envision and experience the provided materials, meditation is not necessary to gain understanding. The instructions and exercises in each chapter are sufficient.

As an alternative, consider one of the many externally oriented mindfulness practices as an alternative, including mindful walking, exercise, or simply observing nature. The instructions and exercises can be reflected upon while engaging in any mindful practice.

During any journey of self-discovery, people are reminded of challenges they are facing or have faced in the past. Because of these challenges and the emotions that come with them, it is important to have access to outside support resources.

Trusted friends, family, spiritual directors or guides, churches, synagogues, temples, and mosques are all sources of emotional, spiritual, and relational support. Individual and group therapeutic resources may be useful. Psychologytoday.com can be a good online resource for connecting with a local therapist.

There are also many free meeting resources that can be found with a little research online and through local churches and community centers. These include grief support, divorce support, child with special needs support, senior support, caretaker support, emotions anonymous, and codependency anonymous just to name a few. Free recovery-oriented meeting resources include AA, NA, Dharma Recovery, Celebrate Recovery, Overeaters Anonymous, Gamblers Anonymous, and others.

Addiction, depression, and other mental health related issues can be deadly if not treated properly. Detox from active substance addiction may require medically assistance to be safe, and clinical depression and other issues may require licensed professional help and medications for a person to become stable enough to benefit from this or any holistic program. This program has not been evaluated by any certification body, and is not meant to diagnose, treat, cure, or prevent any disease.

With all those caveats in mind, the developer of this program is a Spiritual Director and Retired Therapist in Georgia, has Masters Degrees in Theology and Counseling, has worked and authored books and programs used in addiction, homelessness, and Spiritual Development programs.

Narrative

Every person lives on a shoreline between two universes. The land represents the external universe, vast and beautiful, full of wonders and beckoning exploration. The water represents an internal universe, deep and mysterious, also beckoning exploration. With earth below and sky above, a sacred breeze moves across the waters, connecting universes with movement and fragrances from sea to land and land to sea. The sacred breeze animates and inspires the shoreline inhabitants, bringing breath, life, and creative consciousness.

Alive and inspired, the shoreline inhabitants explore their environments and express their creative gifts in myriads of wonderful ways.

Liberation, Love, and Creative Awakening provides a path for exploring the internal mysteries of consciousness, the external mysteries of relationship, and transcendent mysteries of faith. As the journey progresses, practitioners gain clarity, love, self-confidence, and joyful creative expression, which liberates and inspires further exploration and creativity.

Every journey begins with a first step. Welcome.

Life Consciousness, and Creativity:

Many ancient languages recognize two forms of Spirit: Breath or Life Spirit, and Consciousness Spirit. In Hebrew the word for Breath Spirit is *Ruach*, while the word for Consciousness Spirit is *Nephesh*. Likewise, in Greek, life Spirit is *Pneuma*, and Consciousness Spirit is *Psyche*.

All life has material substance and needs both forms of Spirit to survive. Breath provides motion and means for the absorption of nutrients and oxygen and the release of waste. Consciousness provides creativity and motivation for both evolutionary development and use of external resources for improving comfort, lifespan, and the creation of offspring. While breath brings life and animation, consciousness inspires living creatures to move toward light and warmth, toward nutrients, and toward mutually supportive relationships.

The earliest life forms on this planet did not have the ability to breathe and move on their own. The functions of Ruach and Nephesh, breath, and consciousness, were provided by underwater volcano vents (Dodd et al., 2017). The vents provided motion, nutrients, and clearing of waste. As consciousness and the material structure of these life forms evolved with more complexity, life was able to move away from those vents and eventually breathe and seek nutrients and comfort on their own.

The lowliest viruses and the most complex human beings depend on life, breath, breeze, and consciousness. This is even true, to a limited extent, for the formation of crystals. While external elements like wind, water, and pressure provide the Ruach motion for the forming of crystals, the inherent atomic and molecular structures

3

provide the Nephesh creativity for forming crystals. Some crystals, like snowflakes, can grow into unique, complex, and beautiful structures. While chemical properties guide the creative development of crystals, complex life forms develop wondrous and varied creative gifts and relationships.

Every human being carries incredible potential within. The seeds of this potential are creative gifts. When creative gifts are nurtured and cultivated, they blossom into beautiful expressions. Once developed, creative expressions can be shared with and inspirational to others.

The sharing of creative expressions can provide motivation and resources to continue to develop and share more and more creativity. This process of developing and sharing creativity is both self-sustaining and bountiful, producing fruits in quantities tens and hundreds of times greater than the time and resources invested in development.

Creative gifts are unique to every human being, and they extend throughout the range of human experience. From working with hands and materials to creating beautiful and useful art and objects, and working with people to bring comfort and healing, the scope of human creative potential is vast. And when people work together cooperatively, the potential for creative expression and product is almost without limit.

Creative expression is moved by inspiration. At any time in a person's life, creative potential can catch a breeze of inspiration and sail into new and unexplored territory, producing utility, beauty, and healing along the way.

Resources for developing potential are many. Resources are Transcendent and Immanent, and external and internal, originating from others and from within self.

Transcendent means beyond understanding. Transcendence describes the experiences of faith and epiphany. If you ask a composer of any artistic expression where her or his inspiration begins, you will often get the answer, "I don't know, it is a mystery." This is dynamic transcendence in action. The epiphany is the realization of the creative product, and faith helps open a person to the possibility that the inspiration will continue to come, again and again.

Immanent resources are closer at hand, more easily recognized and grasped. The Latin root of the word "human" is *"Humus,"* or earth. Earth-centered, or "grounded" existence gives humanity access to materials to cultivate and to shape from the earth, from seeds and gardens to artistic media and building materials. Grounded existence allows physical motion in dance, exercise, and healing touch. The energy in light and motion of air molecules allows the production of colors and sounds. Humanity's immanent internal resources are neurological, hormonal, flesh, and bone, as well as breath, creative thought, and subconscious dreams.

Immanent resources are also social, in the encouragement of family and friends, instruction from teachers, and the sharing and exchange of creative ideas and products with others. Listening to music, experiencing paintings and sculpture, and marveling at the words written and shared by gifted authors, provide both transcendent and immanent external sources of learning and inspiration. They stimulate something internal; they open the gates to more transcendent inspiration and more creative expression.

Creativity Challenges and Motivation

Even with nurtured creative potential, creative expression can be challenging. People sometimes get stuck, they succumb to depression and anxiety, and addictions and codependent behaviors can hold them back from realizing potential.

Everyone has feelings buried in the deepest parts of their brains that can hold them back from realizing creative potential. For the most part, deep feelings help people to stay safe. They may send a signal to run if a snake or spider is discovered, or they may send a signal to become aggressive if there is potential danger.

But deep feelings also may prevent people from trying new things and taking risks that could be beneficial, like new relationships, new challenges, and new employment opportunities. Sometimes deep feelings hold people back from reaching their potential, and from developing and sharing creative gifts.

Challenging deep and persistent protective feelings or core beliefs, and recognizing new ways to be motivated and to live requires a lot of effort. In fact, challenging protective instinct and allowing growth and blossoming can represent the challenge of a lifetime. To undertake such a monumental task, a person needs a sense that she or he is worth the effort. Undertaking any task of such magnitude requires a belief that the effort is worthwhile.

The good news is that every person is worth the effort. In fact, the worth of every human being is sacred beyond measure. Sacred worthiness means every person is worthy of love, happiness, success, and well-being. This makes physical, mental, emotional, and spiritual self-care worth the time and effort.

Some people are raised to believe that self-care is self-ish. Religious traditions, families, and even occupations send messages that people need to take care of the "other" before taking care of "self." Nothing could be further from the truth. Anyone who has ever flown in an airplane knows that if oxygen masks drop and the person sitting next to them needs help, they need to put their own masks on first. Why? Because without that flow of oxygen to maintain their own waking consciousness, helping others would be impossible.

Self-care goes beyond simply attending to survival needs. Self-care includes development of creative gifts as well. If any healthy individual can help another to put on an oxygen mask, how much more can a trained physician provide help? To develop healing gifts, a physician must commit to self-care and to self-development. The process starts with the creative gifts that may have been present from birth, and continues with reaching out for help and education.

Similarly, crayon drawings from children are beautiful and inspiring, but how much more inspiring are artistic gifts when developed to the level of Van Gogh or Monet?

Humans are creative and social beings. Developing and exercising creative gifts benefits everyone and everything. Humanity, the world, and all of creation needs every human being to develop, exercise, and share each their own creative gifts.

The very survival of humanity may depend on the development of every person's creative gifts. How many Einsteins and Mother Theresas are born every day and never reach their creative potential because of poverty or lack of support? How much would the world benefit if every individual were given the opportunity to develop to his and her fullest creative potential?

While individuals cannot resolve the vast darkness of poverty and conflict that prevent so many people from developing creative potential, with help individuals can begin addressing the darkness that is buried within their own hearts, minds, and beings. Just the act of seeking help and letting go of each individual pocket of darkness has a cascading effect. Unlocking potential, sharing light, optimism, and creative gifts can affect tens, hundreds, and even millions of others in positive ways.

Creative Flow and Mindfulness

Most theistic (God-believing) and nontheistic traditions assert that the end-point for human potential is some sort of static state that is to be reached and rested in. Heaven, Pure Land, the Kingdom, Nirvana, and Paradise are some of the names used to identify this potential. However, Spirit, life, and creativity are dynamic, active, and always in motion. Human consciousness is not a static state to be achieved and rested in, but rather a flow to be engaged. Humanity has the capacity and the opportunity to engage and participate in this "Spiritual flow" here and now.

Sacred writings of many faiths associate Spirit with breath or breeze. Without movement, a breeze quickly becomes stagnant air, and without breath life is lost. Similarly, without movement, a dynamic life of creativity and joy can devolve into a stagnant, oppressive existence.

Stepping into one's creative flow, means allowing one's mind, heart, and flesh to be motivated into expressive motion. How does one step away from any limiting dark stagnation and into creative Spirit flow? There are many possibilities, and many approaches to this problem, but they all start with self-awareness or mindfulness.

A person who is mindfully aware of her or his very human issues, (examples include diabetes, addiction, codependency, or fear of failure), respond by seeking help. People who are not self-aware follow their instincts, trying to make the pain stop, and many times their instincts lead them into avoidant, isolating, or even destructive paths.

How do people develop mindfulness? There are many possibilities. In the book "The Artist's Way," (Cameron, 1992) Julia Cameron recommends journaling to develop mindful self-awareness. In "Purpose Driven Life" (Warren, 2002) Rick Warren describes a faith-based path that includes developing self-awareness through prayer and personal reflection. In the book "Prayer," (Foster, 1992) Richard Foster describes a variety of approaches to prayerfully gain self-awareness. There are literally thousands of books and classes describing various approaches to gaining mindful self-awareness regarding the challenges that hold people back.

Another path that is often utilized and practiced is meditation. In a way, all practices that develop mindfulness are meditative practices, and there are hundreds of techniques, books, classes, and even aps that help people to gain the healthful insights that come with meditation.

Most forms of meditation, including contemplative prayer, are

7

beneficial to engage in, whether for relaxation, for developing mindfulness, or for developing Spiritual connection.

As mentioned in the Preface, this Liberation, Love, and Creative Awakening (LLCA) journey is designed to help people identify and release the sources of suffering in life, and to help discern sacred self-worth and creative gifts. The goal is to live a joyful and fulfilled life, engaging in healthy relationships and sharing creative gifts for the benefit of self and others.

The meditation practices within this program work both internally and externally, developing an appreciation for and connection with both self and others. The practices help a person to form connections in both immanent, grounded human terms and in Transcendent creativity. Knowing and connecting with "self" and "other" is key to this practice, and part of what makes it so powerful.

LLCA meditation might also be described as Tantra-Kaya, which is a combination of two Buddhist terms. Tantra is a discipline or practice used to gain inward insight and strength through releasing desires and releasing attachments to nonpermanent things. Kaya is a term used to represent the emanation of Buddha, or the ways in which Buddha Spirit reaches out to connect with people. Thus, Sacred Breeze uses a Tantra-Kaya approach to release limitations, gain creative insight, and reach out and connect with others both physically and spiritually, in immanent and transcendent ways.

Exercise: Self Affirmation:

Every journey begins with a first step, and in this case, the first step consists of an affirmation.

The affirmation acknowledges a connection with Origin or Higher Power. For nontheists, Origin might be identified as the Universe and Evolution. For Theists, Higher Power might be identified in many ways, including God, Divine Father, Divine Mother, Jesus, Allah, Krishna, Holy Spirit, and Mystery beyond comprehension.

However one's faith or tradition of origin relates to Higher Power, most people acknowledge that humanity is a product of something. Cosmologist Carl Sagan (Andorfer & McCain, 1980), famously described every human as being composed of "star stuff", produced over billions and billions of years of universal development and evolution. Most theistic traditions identify connection between Higher Power and humanity as one of parent with child, which is acknowledged in this affirmation.

The affirmation also acknowledges that human nature is multidimensional. As mentioned earlier, being human means being physically grounded in existence. As spiritual beings, humans are relational and connected with others. And as transcendent beings, humans possess the attributes of breath and life, as well as creative consciousness.

The affirmation, simply stated, is "I am a beloved child of my Origin / Higher Power made in the image of my Origin/ Higher Power: I am Human, I am Transcendent, and I am Spirit."

One could as easily say "I am a beloved product of the Universe," or "I am a beloved child of God," or "I am a sacred Buddha-nature being." The attribute that is common to all expressions is benevolence, as in loving, caring, source of healing and hope. There is a positive energy flow available in which one can experience peace, love, faith, and creative joy.

However one expresses the affirmation, the intention is to acknowledge one's sacred worth, multi-dimensional nature, and potential.

This affirmation serves to remind that you are worth the effort. You are a sacred being, and you are allowed and encouraged to take care of yourself. And you have creative gifts that are worth developing for your benefit and the benefit of others.

Affirmation is a daily practice. Write the affirmation out, and tape it to a bathroom mirror or refrigerator, so you may see it first thing every morning!

Stabilization Practice Preparation:

As stated earlier, there are many mindful practices, and mindful meditation can be conducted in a variety of ways.

All practices have a similar approach, which starts with choosing something to focus on. The focal point serves as a stable reference for the mind to return to when it wanders.

Examples of focal points include candles, beads, prayers, sacred readings, the practice of writing, and mantras. If sitting meditation is not for you, try a practice that is more tactile, like walking, or allowing a raisin to dissolve slowly in your mouth. The feel of the earth under your feet or the changing texture and flavor of the raisin can serve as a focal point to return to.

The focal point referred to throughout this program will be breath. Breath is always with you; you take it with you wherever you go. Breath is the connection with the flow of life, so it is a great place to start.

It has been mentioned that spirit is a multi-dimensional word. In most languages outside of English, the same word is used for spirit and for life-giving breath or energy. In Hebrew the word is "ruach," in Greek "pneuma," in Chinese "chi," in Japanese "ki," and in Tibetan, the word is "lung." Breath, breeze, life, energy; breathing moves air which supports life.

Breath can also be associated with an imagined "safe space" which can be remembered and visualized. For some, a safe space may be a beach at sunrise or sunset; for others it may be near a stream in a forest, or on a mountain top. For many, a safe space may be associated with a room, perhaps at a grandmother's house or in a childhood home. In whatever way safe space is visualized, a conscious connection with breathing can be made.

The amount of time used during the practice is unimportant at first. For some people, sitting still for two minutes can be a great accomplishment. With time, sitting longer becomes easier. Eventually a person will be able to sit for 20 minutes or more during a practice session.

Using a timer can be helpful at first, just to avoid the distraction of wondering how long a person has been sitting.

The practice begins by recognizing outward distractions, and then moves inward to recognizing physical, thought, and emotional distractions.

Acceptance is important in releasing distractions. A person who approaches meditation with a goal of controlling self or outward distractions becomes frustrated quickly. In contrast, acceptance builds familiarity and mindfulness of one's environment, bodily functions, thoughts, and feelings.

Stabilization Practice:

The practice is started by sitting up straight in a chair, or on a cushion on the floor, cross legged or in a half lotus position, whatever is comfortable and upright. The reason for upright posture is to help avoid drifting to sleep during the practice. Although there is no harm in sleeping, (indeed while reclined this practice can help promote sleep), staying awake and alert helps promote the building of mindfulness, or self-awareness regarding the goings on of the inner universe.

And so, with a straight posture, hands resting on knees or however is comfortable, start with noticing what it feels like to breathe. How does it feel for the air to enter your nose and mouth, how cool is the air hitting the back of your throat?

Consciously breathe with your diaphragm, noting how it feels for your stomach to move in and out as you breath. Athletes, opera singers, and martial artists all learn to breathe with their diaphragms, as it maximizes the amount of oxygen taken in.

As you continue to breath, notice how it feels for your lungs to expand. Notice how relaxing it is to exhale. Notice how you flex your breathing muscles to inhale, and relax them to exhale.

As you breathe, you may notice distractions around you. This is OK. The world keeps moving even when you are meditating. You are not trying to control anything. You are just breathing. As you notice distractions, one by one acknowledge them, accept them, and return your attention to your breathing. This is the natural rhythm of meditation. When attention drifts, just accept and return to center.

While accepting external distractions, you may notice little itches and tickles in your body. The number one rule in this journey is to be kind to yourself. If you need to scratch, go ahead and scratch. If you need to cough, go ahead and cough. Simply attend to your own comfort, and return your attention to your breathing.

After attending to the outside distractions, move your attention to internal distractions. As human beings, our brains are always working; we are always thinking and feeling. This is normal, and just as no attempt was made to control outside distractions, internal thoughts will not be controlled either. This practice does not attempt to control, it cultivates acceptance.

Accept your thoughts and feelings as they arise, and then return your attention to your breathing. Do not judge your thoughts and feelings. Simply recognize them, accept them, and continue to breath. Your thoughts are like clouds drifting across the blue sky of your mind; you can watch them drift on by as you continue to breath.

Continue this process of breathing, recognizing when your mind drifts, and bringing your attention back to your breathing for some time. The amount of time will vary. At first, you may only be able to sustain this practice for a few minutes. A few minutes is great because this is a practice, not a prescription. With practice, you will be able to relax and breathe for longer and longer periods.

When you are ready to close the practice, allow yourself to have positive feelings and intentions about yourself. Extend your positive intentions to others who are located physically nearby, including your neighborhood or town. Allow your positive intentions to extent to all local living creatures, trees and animals, and fish in streams.

Extend your positive intentions to include your county or parish, your state or province, your country, and then extend your positive intentions to include the entire world.

Practice Postlude:

During the practice, distracting thoughts provide clues about what is going on in your subconscious. By recognizing and accepting distractions, you naturally gain insight into your inner universe, including your strengths and the challenges that hold you back.

These introductory practices of affirmation and stabilization provide a powerful foundation for gaining self-awareness, self-confidence, and moving forward in life.

2 EXPLORING CONSCIOUSNESS

In the first chapter, the concept of Spirituality is discussed in terms of breath/life and creative consciousness. A set of affirmations that highlight the sacred and multidimensional nature of being human are discussed. Mindfulness is introduced as a means of developing a better understanding of self and overcoming challenges.

In this chapter, the nature of consciousness and identity are explored. Sacred Core is identified as the central defining aspect of identity and consciousness. The practice meditation involves liberating layers of consciousness and identity so that Sacred Core consciousness can be recognized.

Narrative

A parent and child sit on the shore together, waves lapping at their feet. Curious, the child takes a hand full of sand and examines the diverse sparkling colors closely. As gentle waves retreat, holes appear in the sand. The child digs and is delighted to find a small mollusk. As the child ventures further into the water, a small wave brings water up above the child's knees. Surprised, the child turns back to the parent for reassurance. Smiling, the parent hugs the child. Reassured, the child continues to explore.

Secure Attachments

For most people, the quest for understanding "who am I?" becomes especially important at puberty. For some, self-understanding can become a lifetime pursuit. A stable view of "who I

13

am" begins with secure attachments formed during early childhood (Cassidy, Jones, & Shaver, 2013). A child with secure attachment feels free to explore and to play, knowing that a stable environment and loving adults are available to provide safety and a sense of security when needed.

In a perfect world, all children would experience the security of stable childhood environments. In reality, even the best childhood can include chaotic experiences that leave "holes" in the development of identity.

Recognizing sacred self-worth can help fill holes left behind during identity formation. The journey to sacred self-worth begins with building mindful self-awareness. With a stable foundation of self-awareness, a person gains the ability to manage and overcome insecurities and challenges, whatever their source, and to move forward and thrive. In this chapter, identity and human consciousness are presented as a foundation for building mindfulness, and the meditation practice supports increasing mindful self-awareness.

Being Human

Early civilizations imagined humanity being formed from and modeled after Divine Beings. Prior to the emergence of psychology as a science, Egyptians, Zoroastrians, and ancient Greeks recognized differences between mind consciousness and heart and body consciousness. (Lind, 2001). This dualistic thinking carried into the Christian triune representation of Deity: Father, Son, and Spirit. Over the centuries, triune representations of God and humanity have been expressed in many ways. Divinity, Humanity, and Spirit, Transcendence, Immanence, and Relationship, and even Sacred Male, Female, and Sacred Child. While Higher Power as "Sacred Other" will be discussed later, Jewish Scripture affirms the idea that humans are "created in the image of God" (Tanakh, 1985, Gen 1:26).

While early models representing the nature of humanity were often spiritual in nature and tied to Divine Creator Beings, a psychological model of human consciousness became prominent in the early 20th century. Sigmund Freud described aspects of consciousness in triune terms, including Id (instinct), Ego (intentional will) and Super Ego (ethical – moral will) (Freud, 1923). Freud also described human consciousness in terms of dualistic conscious and subconscious thought processes.

Eastern metaphysics informed Integral Theory in describing human consciousness in layers, states, or bodies. Some of the labels used for these "bodies" include Gross, Subtle, Causal, and Nondual (Wilber, 2016, p87). The LLCA Model for consciousness is inspired by Western Spiritual, Eastern Metaphysical, and Freudian models of psychological consciousness.

In the LLCA model Gross Body represents waking Consciousness, and Subtle Body represents the subconscious that is noticeably active during sleep while dreaming. While Eastern Metaphysics associates Causal Body with the origins of creation and the universe, the LLCA model associates Causal with the evolutionary origins of consciousness, including the Id or Instinct and neural responses (instinct can "cause" people to react automatically to certain stimuli). And while Eastern Metaphysics views a Nondual state as a realization of unity with the universe, the LLCA model associates Sacred Core with Superego, or a core Transcendent Body. In the LLCA model, Sacred Core Consciousness exists in nondual communion with the creative origins of the universe. All of this will be unpacked further in later chapters, for now the model is presented as a guide for the journey.

Regardless of the model used, people function as whole beings, with each part operating independently and in harmony with the others. Indeed, bodily functions operate in this manner also. A person is hardly aware of the heart pumping, the stomach digesting, lungs breathing, and neurons firing, and yet there they are, integral parts of every whole functioning human.

The same might be said of the Greco-Christian Triune model, as human, transcendent, and spiritual aspects of Being operate both independently and in harmony. The layers in the consciousness model introduced here also work together independently and in harmony.

Consciousness Model

A diagrammatic representation of human consciousness might look something like this:

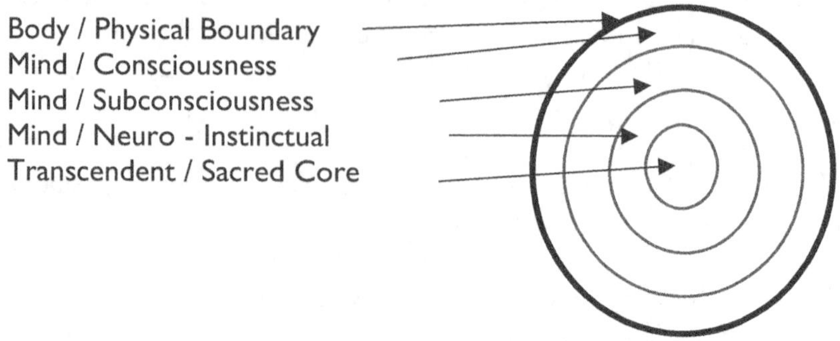

Body / Physical Boundary
Mind / Consciousness
Mind / Subconsciousness
Mind / Neuro - Instinctual
Transcendent / Sacred Core

Figure 1: Whole Being "I Am"

This model of four concentric circles includes a hard physical boundary on the outer ring, representing the physical body. Everything inside the physical boundary is "self," while everything outside the physical boundary is "other."

Consciousness can be understood as an entire universe that begins forming from the earliest stages of fetal development. The first, most primitive layer of consciousness is purely neurological, or instinctual. Early neurological development begins gathering information about what is good, comfortable, and sustaining, and what is bad, uncomfortable, and harmful. Early instinctual beliefs are hard coded into human neurology, or deep within the primitive brain.

The instinct layer of consciousness motivates reaction, because living things know instinctually that safety and well-being require an ability to react to external stimuli. Objects that are extremely hot or cold are avoided, a breast is a source of nourishment and comfort, and early experiences teach that contact outside of self can be either nurturing and joyful or chaotic and frightening.

The next layer to consider in human consciousness is the subconscious. The subconscious can be imagined as an inner model of the outside universe. The subconscious is always working, running simulations that decide whether going down this path or that path will be safe or not. The subconscious model develops as people mature and experience life.

The subconscious also acts as a buffer between the neurological instinct layer and waking consciousness. If the deep primitive brain is activated by interaction with the environment, the subconscious translates those signals into feelings, which waking consciousness recognizes and interprets with thoughts.

In addition to serving as a model of the universe and as a buffer between instinct and consciousness, the subconscious acts as a repository for various ego identities. This concept of ego identity will be explored more fully in the next chapter.

By the time a person reaches puberty and a unified sense of core identity begins to emerge, the inner universe is nearly complete. Conscious thoughts act as an arbiter between the inner subconscious model and the outer universe. If the conditions of the inner and the outer universes do not match, discomfort is experienced. Waking consciousness forms ideas about how to bring the inner and outer universes into alignment. Attempts are made to either manipulate the outside environment or evolve the inner model of the universe to match external experiences.

For example, imagine that a child is exposed to the movie Jaws (Spielberg, Williams & Willams, 1975) at an early age, and the inner universe model forms the belief that the beach is not a safe place to be. If later in life that person is invited to go to the beach with friends, the subconscious may sound an alarm to avoid the experience. In anticipation of the experience the subconscious may reach out in alarming dreams (nightmares), which are remembered by the waking consciousness. The warning is brought to the surface so that waking consciousness can take action to help ensure safety.

On the other hand, if the subconscious inner universe believes the beach is a safe and fun place to visit, dreams of vacations at the beach may help carry a person through school and work days, until a beach vacation is possible. Or, if fortunate, a person may take a career on or near the water, allowing the feelings of joy and fun to be part of day-to-day experience.

This layered model of consciousness is all well and good, but what of the sacred core? If every human has a sacred core, why doesn't everyone develop in a manner that is well adjusted, connected, and joyful? One might say that the sacred core is always there no matter what life's circumstances bring. The sacred core acts as a beacon, or a still, small voice that encourages a person through all circumstances to live, to love, and to thrive.

The sacred core reminds us of our individual and collective creative, loving potential. The sacred core encourages people to grow beyond learned limitations. The sacred core encourages connection with the surrounding universe with relationships and experiences.

Sacred Core is also the source of Creative gifts, that can be developed and shared with others. Sacred Core provides a reminder that every human is sacred, unique, and has creative gifts to share.

While Sacred Core encourages healthy development, self-awareness regarding subconscious and instinctual fears can help a person to learn, accept, and move through perceived challenges. Self-awareness can raise awareness of one's sacred core and help a person to build a conscious identity that celebrates life, love, and creative engagement.

Identity:

Another way to understand the concentric circle model of consciousness is to consider identity. For example, consider how a person may answer the question "who are you?"

A person who is asked "who are you?" may provide an answer based on belonging to a family or group. For example, one might answer "I am the child of my mother and father," or "I am the parent of my children," or "I am the spouse of my partner." In a very real sense, identity is formed based in relationships formed throughout life.

Identity is also influenced from the neurological / instinctual layer of consciousness, through the biological imperative to form physically intimate relationships. In other words, sexual identity is central to human identity. Male, female, gay, or straight, the biological imperative is not solely for procreation; it influences who people are attracted to and connect with intimately.

Sexual identity is not a choice, but rather is tied into neurological instinct and even deeper, into the sacred core identity. (Later chapters describe a congruence or correlation between the neurological instinct layer and the energies that flow within the Sacred Core.)

Identity is also associated with "I believe" statements. In a way, "I believe" statements are relational, as they are learned and formed through relationships. People initially connect with faith traditions through culture and ethnicity, and with political convictions through exposure to societal norms. Sometimes referred to as "core beliefs," immature and unrealistic convictions developed during early childhood can change and adapt with time and experience.

In Western culture especially, identity has been strongly connected with "doing," as related to occupation or career. From this perspective, if someone is asked "Who are you?" the response might be "I am a brick layer," or "I am a delivery driver," or "I am a physical therapist" for example.

The "I Do" aspect of identity grows from the development and sharing of creative gifts that originate within the Sacred Core. Creative gifts vary across a spectrum of possibilities that include social, artistic, and practical skills.

Another layer of identity that lies close to the physical boundary is the "I have" layer. The "I have" or "I enjoy" aspect of identity can hold great importance, and can help contribute to a view of self that is consistent with every layer in the circle.

For example, a person who enjoys fishing or hunting generally owns the equipment associated with those pastimes, as a hobby or as an occupation. A person with a consistent identity that fulfills all layers might say "I have fishing equipment, I do fishing, I enjoy fishing, and fishing was part of my relationship with my parents." Any creative interest could be equally fulfilling across all layers, for example "I have oil paints and brushes, I create paintings, I love to paint landscapes, and I share my paintings and skills with others," supports an identity that says, "I am an artist who works in oil paint media."

Remember that creativity is part of humanity's sacred core and mission, which is to develop and share creative potential in a way that benefits self and others. Joy in life comes not only from connecting with creative potential, but also from engaging and sharing with others.

These aspects of identity – being, belonging, believing, doing, and having, may also be represented graphically:

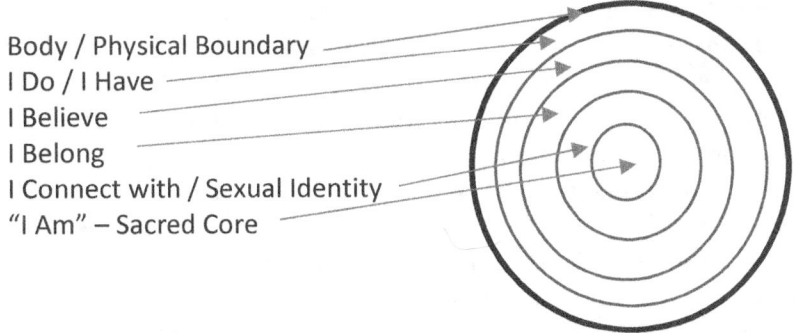

Body / Physical Boundary
I Do / I Have
I Believe
I Belong
I Connect with / Sexual Identity
"I Am" – Sacred Core

Figure 2: Identity "I Am"

Exercise:

As an exercise in building mindfulness, it would be helpful to draw concentric circles and fill in aspects of your own identity, including your understanding of your creative core. There are several aspects within each area of identity to consider. Brainstorm and jot them all down at first, and then later consider ranking them in terms of how closely you identify with them. For example, in the "I Do" layer, someone may have an occupation as a delivery driver, enjoy cooking as a creative hobby, and also engage in parenting, bike riding, and reading. Upon reflection, this person may decide she or he identifies most closely with parenting, followed by cooking, etc.

Keep in mind that identity can change over a lifetime. For example, as a person matures, or as children grow and leave the household, the "I Do" identity will likely shift in another direction, perhaps toward a hobby or volunteer activity for example. Being self-aware can help make the transition easier.

Like the previous consciousness model, this identity model has a physical boundary where outside the physical "self" lies "other." The way people relate to "other" is through "relationship." In future chapters, the consciousness model is extended to include healthy relationships.

Identity Archetypes

Identity theorists have hypothesized that for each aspect of identity, a person also holds an internal standard or ideal associated with that identity (Burke and Stets, 2009). These ideal archetypes are part of the inner subconscious universe, and are formed through learning from external social sources. For example, the archetype for an occupation might be codified in a job description, a professional ethical standard, and / or a societal norm.

Societal norms come in many forms. Parents tell children that to meet a "well behaved" standard, they need to be respectful, quiet, and good students. Advertisements entice people to buy products based on how the product will help them to conform to an ideal, be it an ideal woman who looks and smells a certain way, an ideal man who participates in masculine activities, or an ideal parent who purchases certain foods and products for child care.

Over time, ideals and standards get internalized, becoming part of a person's subconscious model for self and the universe. Internalized models also evolve over time based on education and experience. For example, a person who carries an identity that includes an activity like fishing will learn over time what kinds of equipment, bait, and techniques work for specific geographical areas and species. Similarly, preferences in clothing, hygiene products, and perhaps cosmetics may develop over time to create a certain look, feel, and smell associated with identity.

Of course, there can be quite a bit of difference between societal ideals and reality. Everyone is different. If internalized ideals based on societal norms are not realistic, a great deal of stress can be experienced. A student who has an internalized "A plus" grade standard and gets a "B" grade may experience a great deal of stress. Body image issues are distressingly common among young women, due to unrealistic advertised societal norms.

Archetypes that are too strict or too well defined tend to stifle creativity. For example, a "cover band" who strives to accurately reproduce the sounds and mannerisms of Elvis or The Beatles exercises creativity and talent, but may not compose their own music. To do so would violate the established standard.

Identity standards can serve as inspiration or as the opposite, stagnation. For example, parents may unintentionally project thoughts that say "that kid can't do anything right." Over time the standard of "doing nothing right" can become part of one's subconscious identity model, contributing to low self-esteem.

Developing awareness of identity archetypes, both positive and negative, is important. Remember that identities evolve over time, so self-awareness regarding identity standards can help move the development process in a positive and creative direction. In later chapters the process of connecting with a joyful and creative Sacred Core identity will be explored. The task at hand within this chapter is developing awareness and acceptance of existing identity strengths and challenges.

Understanding identity influences can also enable liberation from standards that restrict creative development. In this section's meditation practice, efforts are made to release some of the learned idealized characteristics described above. The practice establishes a deeper mindfulness as to which aspects of identity are motivating, and which aspects hold a person back from experiencing joy, and developing and sharing creativity.

Awareness, acceptance, and letting go of negative internalized standards are a repeated theme over the next couple chapters. Throughout this process, a space for personal evolution is being created, so that new and better experiences become possibilities that may not have been considered previously.

Practice:

This practice moves through a process of imagining the release of layers of consciousness, like peeling away the layers of an onion. The process of considering and releasing layers of consciousness creates a self-awareness of the existence and function of the layers. The journey through outer layers of consciousness leads to the Sacred Core.

For this part of the practice, begin with the familiar breath centered stabilization described in chapter 1. At this point, mind stabilization should be getting easier. If you have been able to sit quietly with your breathing for 10-20 minutes, you are ready to engage this practice.

Sitting with straight posture, breathing with the diaphragm, start by accepting and letting go of external distractions that affect your comfort. Kindness to self is still the number one rule, so attend to your discomforts as they arise.

Next, turn attention to internal distracting thoughts and feelings, and using breath, consciously accept and let them go as well. As distractions arise, return your attention to your breathing. Remember to associate your breath with a safe space.

Once thoughts are stable, try visualizing yourself as a tree trunk with a series of concentric rings. Your sacred core occupies the heart of the trunk, and extends from your head, through your heart and core center, to the base on which you are rooted.

Your skin is represented by the bark of the tree, and the outermost ring contains waking consciousness. This layer of consciousness extends through your entire body as well, from your head to your root. Waking consciousness includes recognition of both brain and body experiences.

Once you recognize waking consciousness as your outermost ring, imagine releasing the ring, which exposes the next deeper ring. If you like, it may help to surrender your waking consciousness to a Higher Power you can trust, or simply imagine yourself letting go.

Breath is the Sacred Breeze that connects you with Spirit and the Universe. With every exhale allow yourself to surrender waking thoughts. With every inhale, imagine peace entering and flowing throughout your body. With every breath, your waking thoughts become quieter, and a sense of peace develops.

After several breaths, turn your attention to the next deeper concentric ring of your identity, the subconscious. When conscious thought is surrendered, the subconscious can bring forth feelings, and sometimes dream like visions. You may recognize identities that are part of your life being activated, from childhood and from throughout your life. Feelings and visions can be associated with identities that are part of your subconscious.

As these feelings, visions, and identities arise, recognize also a sense of compassion for them. As you accept the feelings, visions, and associated identities, imagine releasing and liberating them. Again, you may surrender them to the care of your trusted and benevolent Higher Power. With every exhale, allow feelings to dissipate, and with every inhale experience liberation and peace.

Gradually, a quiet sense of peace takes over, and a sense of true rest sets in. This may be your first time experiencing this sort of peace, which may startle you back into conscious thought. This is OK. This is natural. Just continue the process of breathing.

The process of touching and releasing the subconscious self can elicit buried treasures and challenges, or thoughts and feelings that have not been considered for many years. If uncomfortable feelings or memories arise, be kind to yourself and return your attention to your breathing and your safe space. If necessary, discontinue the practice. With the help of trusted others, negative feelings can be processed later in a safe environment. As thoughts and feelings are surrendered, eventually the space to experience inspiration and creativity is realized.

If you feel safe continuing the practice, rest in the space and freedom that comes with release of subconscious feelings. After some period of rest, recognize an even deeper ring in your consciousness, your deep neurological instinct.

Safety and self-care are important at this layer of consciousness. As you surrender yourself at the neurological instinct level, you need to both feel and be safe. At this point it may be helpful to surrendering your instincts to a trusted, unconditionally loving Higher Power. During this process, there is only you, your breath, and your Higher Power.

As you breathe, and as thoughts and feelings arise as they naturally do, recognize how deeply affecting they can be. Recognize instinctual feelings of pleasure and fear. At this level, humans are purely reactive, and basic survival experiences and reactions are in play. One by one, recognize these deep reactive instinctual feelings, and with every exhale accept and surrender them. Every inhale reinforces feelings of safety and peace.

If at any time you feel uncomfortable, feel free to break away from the practice. Continue to breathe and consider your safe space. Above all, be kind to yourself. If you feel comfortable enough to continue, take a moment to rest in the growing sense of safety and peace.

After visualizing the release of the instinct layer of your consciousness, you may recognize the next deeper level, the Sacred Core of existence. Like an eternal flame, fueled by life and pure transcendent consciousness, your sacred core is not static, but in motion, flowing, and coursing through you. Like a sacred breeze, its flow is ever present, unceasing, eternal. From branches to root, sacred consciousness flows, and from root to branches, sacred life flows. Every breath brings life, cleansing, and strength.

Stepping into your sacred core, you feel alive and liberated. You may have a sense that you are somehow outside of space and time, and outside the rigors of physical existence. Still rooted and grounded in your living, breathing humanity, you are also connected with your transcendent, creative being; you are fully present. With every breath, experience pure existence.

After some time dwelling within your sacred core, begin to emerge from this meditation with gratitude. Gratefully acknowledge yourself, the sacred nature of who you are, and your trusted Higher Power. Also gratefully acknowledge others, including people you know and love, friends and acquaintances, and every human being. Gratefully acknowledge all living creatures, including animals and plants, and gratefully acknowledge the gift of creation. From the smallest subatomic particle to the vast universe, you are part of something wonderful.

After the practice is completed, making notes in a diary can be helpful for remembering and tracking progress in your experience. Release of consciousness is the beginning of healing and liberation, and seeking outside help and guidance from trusted family, friends, clergy, or a mental health therapist may be part of the healing process. Much of the work and benefit that arises from meditation occurs between sessions, so take advantage of your emerging self-awareness and seek help in processing the experience.

It is OK if the practice was interrupted. The interruption can also be journaled and discussed with trusted others. Like all parts of this practice, the process develops mindful self-awareness. You are learning to recognize and accept the forces within yourself that both challenge and motivate you.

It is also OK if the process feels too uncomfortable to repeat. Continue with the breath centered mind stabilization, which is powerful and healing as a stand-alone practice.

If the process was comfortable enough to try again, repeat this exercise, every other day if possible. The more you practice meditation, the easier the practice gets, as it prepares you for the next phase which is true, complete self-emptying.

3 CORE ENERGY CENTERS

In Chapter 2, the concept of secure attachment is discussed as foundation for mindful self-awareness. Identity models are also described from ancient Western, Eastern, and Psychology origins.

The "consciousness plane" is introduced. Based on a Buddhist / Integral model, the consciousness plane is described as a system of concentric circles, identifying layers of conscious self. In the center of the consciousness plane, the Sacred Core breath / life and creative consciousness spiritual energies flow.

Consistent with consciousness model, an identity awareness model is introduced along with an exercise in developing self-awareness. Identity standards are discussed as models that guide relationships and behaviors.

The Chapter 2 practice consists of releasing outer layers of consciousness to connect with the Sacred Core.

In this chapter, the Buddhist concept of attachment is discussed. The consciousness model is expanded into three dimensions to include chakras or energy centers. Holistic synergies between chakra energy and physical neurotransmitters are explored. The connection between core energy centers, neurotransmitters, and addictive behaviors are also discussed.

Narrative:

The young man was raised as royalty in a sheltered, comfortable, and secure environment. One day the young man wandered outside the family compound, leaving behind the comforts and perhaps addictions of a royal lifestyle. Being a sensitive person who was sheltered from the rigors of life, he was shocked by the amount of suffering he observed outside the palace gates. People were sweating and suffering as they toiled to cultivate crops. Wildlife was being disrupted and harmed as part of the cultivation process. Dismayed, he left the safety of the compound and engaged in a period of answer seeking. After enduring a great deal of suffering in his quest for insight, he sat under a spreading Bodhi tree and began to meditate. Eventually the young man was blessed with insight into the nature of human suffering. His insight was that suffering comes from desire or attachment to impermanent things.

Human Suffering: A Buddhist Perspective

In the Chapter 2, the concept of "secure attachment" is discussed as a part of healthy childhood development. Secure attachment allows a child to explore and play and learn with a sense of security. The internalized security developed in childhood allows a healthy person to continue to learn and grow throughout a lifetime.

During childhood development, secure attachment might be viewed as a safety tether that provides a sense of security.

While secure attachment is a healthy part of childhood development, lack of secure attachment during childhood can lead to seeking security in unhealthy ways. In Buddhist philosophy, attachments or desires are considered the source of all suffering. Unhealthy attachments described in Buddhist philosophy can be traced back to lack of secure attachment during childhood development.

To understand Buddhist philosophy, knowing a little about the history of Buddhism is helpful (Harvey, 1990). The young man described in the opening narrative is Siddhartha Gautama Buddha, who was born in about 480 BC in India. The narrative provides a brief description of his life story, through which Buddhist philosophy originated.

From a Buddhist perspective, unhealthy attachments can be broken down into the "three poisons of Buddhism," (Buswell, 2013) namely attachments, aversions, and ignorance.

Many people spend much of their lives chasing after some things, and running away from others. For the most part, people are not aware they are doing this. Chasing just seems to be a part of their identity and provides motivation for day-to-day activities. Examples of things that people chase, or are attached to, include money, relationships, security, safety, attention, and substances such as alcohol and drugs. The list goes on.

Examples of aversions, or things people run away from, include unsafe situations, fear of failure, fear of success, fear of being judged, and fear of poisonous creatures like spiders and snakes. Again, the list goes on and on.

Ignorance, the third poison, is just being unaware of the chase as it is going on. For the most part, people react to situations based on the poisons they carry in their consciousness. People react to attachments by trying to fill any voids that are present. A good example of this is turning to unhealthy relationships for fulfillment, which is known as codependency. Substances, gambling, excessive eating, and excessive work also represent addictive forms of attachment.

Reaction to fears may seem obvious, but they may manifest in delayed and subtle ways. Fear of success may manifest as quitting jobs just as success seems possible or even inevitable. Relationships are ended when they start feeling too close or intimate. Fear of failure can also manifest in not even trying, or not completing tasks because the efforts seem "just not good enough."

All these "poisons" motivate reaction, as opposed to intentional action. A person who is aware of internal poisons or challenges can recognize the challenges as sources of motivation, which can lead to intentional actions. Motivation will be discussed much more in later chapters.

Sacred Core Energy

Recall the consciousness plane introduced in chapter 2, consisting of concentric rings that represent Sacred Core, instinct, subconscious, and waking consciousness layers. Expanding the model into a third dimension, one might visualize the sacred core as a column through which flows the sacred spiritual energies that are the essence of life and consciousness.

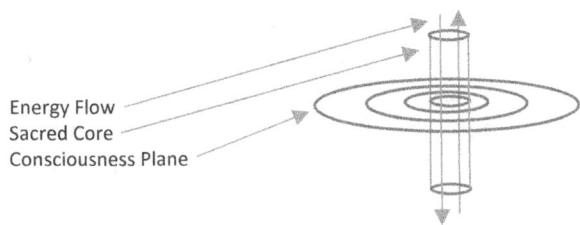

Energy Flow
Sacred Core
Consciousness Plane

Figure 3: Expanded Consciousness

It was mentioned in chapter 1 that when referring to Spirit as the source of life, many languages use the same word for Spirit, breath, and breeze. This makes sense as breathing is a good indication of life. In Hebrew, the word for breath, spirit, life, and breeze is "ruach." In Hebrew Scripture, when God breathed the breath of life into the dust, it was the 'ruach' of God that animated the dust into living creatures (Tanakh, 1985 Gen 2:7).

The Greek the word for breath, breeze, and Spirit is "pneuma." The Greek word is familiar as the root of the word "pneumatic," which describes tools and machines that use air pressure for power. "Prana" in Sanskrit, and "lung" in Tibetan are other words describing breath, breeze, and Spirit, while Chi in Chinese and Ki in Japanese describe vital life energy.

Breath and breeze have the properties of being in motion and flowing. Without flow, there is no breeze, just static air. Energy in motion makes the presence of breath, breeze, and Spirit known. Christian scripture describes Spirit like the wind, coming and going as she pleases (NRSV, 1989 John 3:8). She cannot be seen, but her presence can be felt through her dynamic motion.

Chakra Energy Centers

The Sacred Breeze of life courses through every living thing. Similarly, the sacred energy of consciousness flows. In Buddhism, Tantra is an "energy aware" discipline or practice used to gain inward insight. In Tantric practice, consciousness energy is recognized as being concentrated in specific locations within the body. These areas of energy concentration are known as chakras. (Yeshe, 2001)

While traditionally seven chakras are recognized, for the purpose of this practice four will be focused on, namely the mind, the heart, the core, and the root.

Chakras can be centers of both positive and negative energy. While positive energy is productive, negative energy literally sucks or depletes a person. When generating energy, chakras bring health and vitality. When draining energy, chakras lose health and vitality and bring suffering. Chakra energy loss manifests in attachments and aversions.

For this practice, the mind chakra is the center of clarity and creativity. When sourcing energy, the mind chakra creates a general sense of well-being. This sense of well-being is often noticed by others in relationships, and people are drawn to positive, hopeful energy. When draining energy, the mind is prone to judgement, confused and an uncomfortable. A sense that "something is not right" is present, and others can sense that as well. Sometimes confusion and discomfort manifests in judgement toward self and others.

The heart chakra is, of course, the center of love. When sourcing energy, a positive feeling of love is felt and shared with others. When draining energy, the heart fosters feelings of resentment. Resentments are a manifestation of unhealthy attachments. Relationships that have "strings attached" often foster resentments over time. Particularly in western culture, people confuse love with attachment. Saying "if you love me, you would do this and that for me" is not love; it is emotional extortion. Real love is love without attachment, or unconditional. Real love says "no matter what, I love you."

Another way to look at heart-based energy is in terms of neediness. If a relationship is established based on neediness, it becomes a burden, draining energy. On the other hand, a relationship based on "love without attachment" is mutually supportive and exudes positive energy.

The core chakra is located just below the diaphragm muscles below the rib cage. The core chakra is the center of confidence, faith, and wisdom. When sourcing energy, self-confidence can be sensed by others, and people tend to be drawn toward self-confidence. When draining energy, the core is the center where fears and burdens reside. Burdens weigh people down, impeding the flow of creative energy, and fears hold people back from even trying to express themselves creatively.

Finally, the root chakra, which is located at the base of the spine, is the center of joy, motivation, and creative enthusiasm. An abundance of root chakra energy stimulates creativity. When draining energy, the core chakra can be the source of addictive obsessions that distract and use up joy and creative energy. Addictions may feel like sources of energy at first, but soon addictions dominate and take over everything. Obsessions can be the result of attachments or aversions, as obsessive behaviors often stem from feelings of insecurity and fear.

Transcendent Consciousness Energy

Bringing the chakras into the core consciousness model would look something like this:

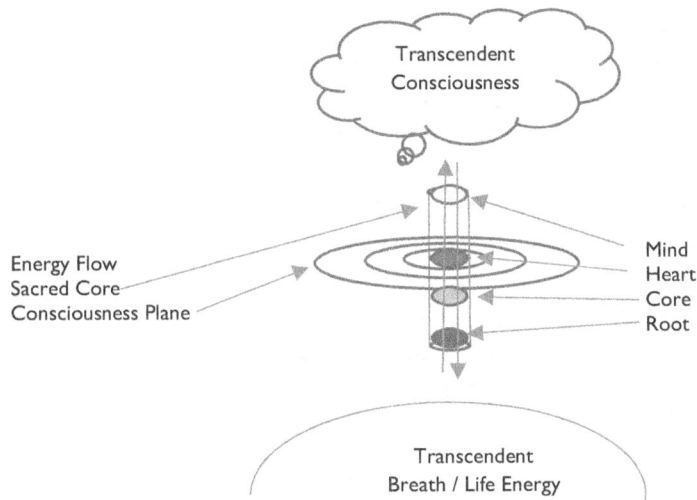

Figure 4: Chakra Energy Centers

One might visualize every living person as a column of consciousness energy. The upper reaches of the model can be thought of as "Transcendent Consciousness," which is an outside source for creative energy. The lower reaches can be thought of as "Transcendent Life Energy," which is also sourced from outside. In the monotheistic Judeo-Christian-Islamic traditions, both transcendent consciousness and life energies come from a single Divine source.

When consciousness energy extends between persons, relationships occur. Relationships will be explored much further in later chapters.

Chakras Synergy with Consciousness

Within the consciousness model, metaphysical energies sourced from chakras can influence all layers of consciousness. In the instinct layer of consciousness, neurochemicals are naturally produced that are associated with each chakra energy center. While neurochemicals are produced within the brain and throughout the human body, it is convenient to associate specific neurochemicals with specific chakras. (Hanson & Mendius, 2009)

For example, creativity associated with the mind chakra is also associated with endocannabinoid neurotransmitters. Clarity of mind is also associated with the neurochemical dopamine.

The feeling of love, or close connection, is associated with both the heart chakra and the neurochemical oxytocin.

A sense of peace and tranquility is associated with both the core chakra and the neurochemical serotonin.

The root chakra is associated with ecstatic epiphany and bursts of joyful expression, which are also associated with endorphins. Endorphins are also natural pain relievers.

These five neurochemicals, namely Endocannabinoid, Dopamine, Oxytocin, Serotonin, and Endorphins, can be abbreviated EDOSE.

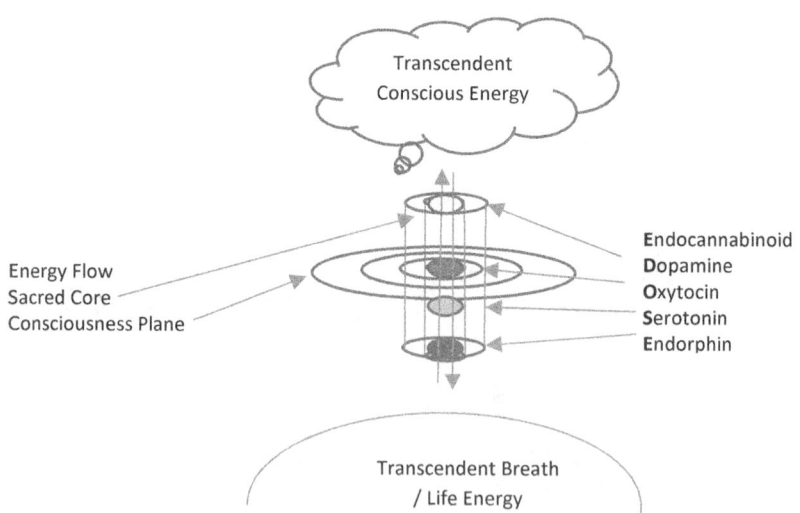

Figure 5: Neurochemicals in Consciousness Plane

The influence of Sacred Core energy centers extends beyond the instinct layer into subconscious and waking consciousness layers. Mind centered energy creates an optimistic outlook in the subconscious that cultivates creative ideas in waking consciousness. The same can be said of heart centered love energy, core centered faith and self-confidence, and root centered joy and enthusiasm, which each cultivate thoughts and actions in the waking consciousness.

Neurochemicals and Addiction

For every naturally produced neurochemical, there are chemical substances that can artificially induce or enhance the effects of naturally occurring neurochemicals when ingested. These externally produced substances can be highly addictive.

While doctor supervised administration of some substances may be helpful for specific and perhaps acute maladies, the human body was not meant to endure long term exposure to external substances. Prolonged exposure to external substances has the effect of reducing the body's ability to respond to naturally occurring neurochemicals. The influence of chakra energy centers is supplanted by external influences. Eventually, the neuroreceptors that respond to naturally occurring neurochemicals become numb due to the added influence of external substances, and more and more of the external substances are required to obtain any desired effect. The trap for addiction is set.

Marijuana and psychedelic substances can produce enhanced feelings of creativity. Psychedelics can reduce the mind's ability to respond to naturally occurring endocannabinoids.

Stimulants, like cocaine, nicotine, and caffeine, can provide an enhanced sense of clarity and well-being. Stimulants reduce the mind's ability to respond to naturally occurring dopamine.

People also engage and remain in unhealthy codependent relationships for a sense of sustained connection. Healthy relationships that naturally produce oxytocin become hard to develop and maintain.

Alcohol and other depressants may induce relaxation as well as euphoria. Pain killers and opioids can produce raw feelings of euphoria that are difficult to escape. These external substances interfere with the body's ability to produce and respond to naturally occurring serotonin and endorphins.

Codependency may be considered a nonchemical addiction, as can behaviors like theft, gambling, sex, and thrill seeking. Nonchemical addictions create surges of dopamine, endorphins, and other neurochemicals within the body that can also be difficult to escape. Both nonchemical and chemical addictions flood the system with neurochemicals at a level that normal healthy activities, like creative expression and healthy relationships, cannot match.

Over time, the enhanced sensations get replaced by raw need (i.e. physical and psychological attachment and dependence) that can destroy a person's life and relationships. One goal of this practice is to recognize and appreciate naturally produced sensations associated with sacred core energies while releasing attachments to unhealthy activities and substances.

Exercise: Dominant Chakras

Given the described characteristics of chakras, neurotransmitters, and energy, here is a mindful exercise to try. Considering your own creative process, which chakra would you say is your dominant "go to" for motivation and creativity? How would you rank your chakras in terms of how they influence you?

Mind centered people tend to think and sometimes overthink when faced with a challenge. Heart centered people, motivated by love, tend to follow their hearts, which sometimes get bruised in the process. Core centered people tend to operate on "gut instinct," reacting and "doing before thinking," Then there are root centered people, who tend to be free spirited and impulsive.

While core centered people tend to react, root centered people tend to act out in ways that provoke reaction from others. Fun and capricious, root centered people have the spark to initiate creativity, but the sparks often fade quickly and working through a creative project to completion can be a challenge.

There are no right or wrong answers here, just self-awareness. Are you mind-centered, heart-centered, core-centered, or root-centered? If you were to rank which centers are dominant, how would you rank them top to bottom?

Chakra energy centers and associated neurochemicals strongly influence how feelings and imagination play out in the subconscious, and how waking thoughts are colored. For example, a heart chakra that is clogged up with resentments would affect how a person thinks and feels, and how a person interacts with others. On the flip side, having a strong sense of unconditional love energy flowing in one's heart also translates into positive instincts, feelings, thoughts, and relationships.

From inner sacred core to outside relationships, chakra energies and corresponding neurochemicals affect how people experience life, relationships, and the world.

Now, imagine living a life where all energies are predominantly productive, where occasionally arising negative energies are mindfully accepted, and creative positive energies are cultivated and shared. This is what this program and the practices are working toward.

Practice:

The Tantric process of self-emptying provides another step in the journey toward cultivating productive energies. During the last practice, layers of consciousness were released one after another until thoughts were centered in the creative core. This practice continues the process by emptying the chakras of negative energy.

In this context, emptiness means a state of complete, unfiltered observation. Sitting in a state of complete emptiness means subjective filters are not engaged in interpreting experiences. It is as if light and sound pass right through a person. Presence and existence are recognized, but experiences are not filtered nor interpreted. Things that might have been distractions before are simply present. Existence becomes lighter than air, with no need for interpretation or control. Everything just is. Complete emptiness is a space of peace, a place of pure unfiltered being.

In tantric practice, the goal of self-emptying is to release the ego. In this Sacred Breeze practice, ego can be understood as subconscious identities. Complete emptiness also means being able to observe and release ego-identities without judgement. When ego-identities are liberated, all that remains is pure existence.

At first, the idea of self-emptying and releasing ego-identities can be daunting and even scary. After all, depression is often described as a feeling of emptiness as well. But depression is more of a burdened emptiness: lonely, alone, and dark. A truly self-emptied state is anything but alone and dark. A self-emptied state is completely present, and the separation between "self" and "universe" is diminished. Tantric masters describe emptiness in terms of feeling at one with everything, as the differences between "self" and "other" seem to melt away.

During this practice, some people find it useful to engage with a "Higher Power." Doing so makes the practice into a kind of meditative prayer. Prayerful words like "I surrender my attachments unto thee, Oh Lord" can be used. Some people find this comforting, and consistent with monotheistic beliefs and cultures.

Sometimes visions occur during self-emptying. Visions can serve to increase mindful self-awareness of processes taking place in the subconscious. Visions may also be an indication of drifting into sleep. Rather than engaging the practice while laying down or slumped into a comfortable chair, consider making the effort to sit up straight, either forward on a chair or on a cushion cross legged on the floor.

****

Begin the practice, as always, with a comfortable upright posture and diaphragm centered breathing. With practice, breathing becomes natural, along with letting go of external distractions, and letting go of internal distractions. Whenever distractions arise, return attention to your breathing.

After releasing distractions, move through the process of releasing your consciousness. Going through the concentric rings, release your waking conscious thoughts, subconscious feelings and ego identities, and your reactive instinctual feelings. Find yourself again in the space of your sacred core, experiencing the sacred flow of existence. You might imagine that transcendent consciousness energy passes from beyond your mind through your core and downward, while transcendent life-breath energy passes from beneath your root through your core and upward.

Now imagine the space where your mind lies. This is the space between your ears, and behind your eyes. As you breath, allow your mind to be cleansed with every inhale, and allow negative energy to be released with every exhale. Imagine your physical breath sweeping into the space where our mind exists, bringing with it cleansing and healing. Recognize how much confusion and judgement exists in your mind. With every exhale, let go of confusion and judgement. Recognize that as you release confusion, you create a space for clarity and creativity. If doing so is helpful, gently offer any confusion and judgement up to your Higher Power with every breath.

Continue this process for several minutes.

Once your mind is in a state of peace, move your imagination down to your heart. The heart is the place where attachments and resentments lie. For many people, the heart becomes scarred and hardened over time. These scars are a result of engaging in love with attachments, whereas pure, unconditional love brings only healing. When letting go of attachments, you create a space for love without attachments, love that is unconditional, love that just is.

As you breathe, every inhale softens your heart, softens scar tissue, and gently pries apart the knots that build up over time. With every exhale, attachments and resentments are released. If doing so is helpful, gently offer your resentments and attachments up to your Higher Power.

In Buddhist philosophy, desire, or attachment to impermanent things, is the source of all suffering. Relationships change. People get older. Jobs come and go, and material objects wear out and need repair. This is the nature of reality. Nothing physical is permanent, and clinging to impermanent things is a futile endeavor. With every breath, recognize impermanence experienced in life, and practice letting go. As you release desires, attachments, and resentments, you create a space in your heart for unconditional love.

Continue this process for several minutes.

After spending some time breathing through and releasing attachments, move attention down to your core which is located below the diaphragm. The core is the center of aversions, or fears and burdens. Realistically, you may recognize that when this meditation is complete, there will still be a mortgage, rent and car payments, and life will go on. But for now, letting go of fears and burdens provides a mini-vacation, and a sense of peace. Consider surrendering your fears and burdens to your Higher Power.

With every inhale experience cleansing and healing; with every exhale recognize the dissipation of the darkness associated with fears and burdens. You may recognize some deep-seated fears refusing to let go. The beginning of all healing is acceptance. Being human includes insecurities. Simply accepting past mistakes, future worries, and your humanity is the beginning of loosening these burdens.

This exercise creates a space for peace, for faith in self, and for faith in your Higher Power, allowing you to release things that are outside your control. A space is also created for wisdom to grow. As fears and burdens are released, the wisdom gained from experience is freed to support faith. Imagine that with every inhale light enters your core, illuminating the dark spaces where fears hide. With every exhale, fears and burdens continue to loosen until they are released.

Continue this process for several minutes.

After spending time releasing fears and burdens, move your attention down to the root chakra located at the base of the spine. This is the center of joy and passion which motivates creative activity. As humans, we love these feelings and experiences. In fact, we love them so much, we sometimes become obsessed with them.

Authentic joy, passion, and creativity are not ends unto themselves. Authentic joy works in dynamic harmony with the entire sacred core. Authentic joy experiences satisfaction in accomplishment. Authentic joy lives in relationship and sharing. Authentic joy engages the intellect with clarity and purpose.

And so, imagine the space at the base of your spine that your root chakra occupies. With every inhale, imagine your breath sweeping in to cleanse any obsessive needs and behaviors. With every exhale, imagine letting go of any neediness and obsessive emptiness that distracts from authentic joy. Every inhale brings cleansing and healing; every exhale brings freedom.

Continue this process for several minutes.

Having liberated consciousness and released negative chakra energies, you may start to develop new way of perceiving yourself and the world. Sounds, light, and vibrations that surround you are no longer distracting. You find yourself in a space of complete observation, as if the sound, the light, and even the air passes through you. You simply bear witness to this. There is no judgement, no need to process. There is just experience. Completely empty, and fully present, you are a part of all the things you experience. The earth below, the sky above, creation all around, as well as life, Spirit, and Consciousness coursing through and all around you. Observe, experience, and become a part of all that is.

At peace now, you begin to emerge from this practice, one breath at a time, with gratitude and joy. Experience positive feelings directed toward yourself, your neighbors, and your loved ones. Experience positive feelings toward the nature and creation that is around you. Expanding outward, allow positive feelings to arise toward everyone and everything in your local town and county or parish, your state or territory, and the country in which you reside. Allow a sense of gratitude to rise up, and allow positive feelings to expand to include everyone on the planet, all living creatures, and all of creation.

And slowly, with great peace and gratitude, emerge from your meditation.

4 PAIN RELIEF AND HEALING

In Chapter 3, sacred core energy centers are discussed in relationship to both productive and negative energy flow. The healthy and restorative nature of productive energy is discussed, as well as the effects of negative draining energy. Chakra energy centers are introduced, as is the connection between energy center flow and neurotransmitter activity. In the practice, chakra centered negativity is released to create a space for well-being, love, self-confidence, wisdom, and creative joy.

In this chapter, the phenomenon of pain is discussed. Pain can be physical, emotional, and even spiritual in nature. Concepts that are explored include sensitivity and resilience, acute vs chronic pain, suffering and attachment, and a spiritual energy model for understanding and managing pain. The practice builds on the previous practice of releasing negative energy for the purpose of releasing pain.

Narrative

There it was again. The headache, starting as a slow throb behind her left eye. She knew from experience what was to come. The steady throb would gradually increase and eventually bring nausea that would distract her from all else. She also knew the sinking feeling in the pit of her stomach. More and more, the sinking feeling and the headaches came together. At first the sinking feeling came with work related stress. At some point, the sinking feeling came in anticipation of the headache pain to come. She had been to her doctor and received medications that helped relieve the pain. They helped, but they also made her tired. Knowing that the medications were there if the pain persisted, she found a quiet place to sit and closed her eyes. Focusing on her breathing, she applied the meditation techniques she had learned. She applied the techniques to the physical pain, and then the emotional pain she was experiencing. The techniques were not very different from the Lamaze practice she had learned during her pregnancy. After several minutes of focused breathing, the pain subsided enough that she could return her attention to her task at hand.

Physical Pain

Physical pain, of course, occurs when the physical body receives an injury of some kind. Neurons send signals of the injury to the brain, which interprets the injury as pain. This injury-pain mechanism activates all levels of consciousness. Instinct / neurological consciousness sends the signal that fight, flight, or freeze may be necessary. Protection identities may also emerge from instinct. The subconscious also activates ego identities familiar with pain, and the subconscious model of the universe provides a map for planning the next move in response to pain. Waking consciousness, having received the message that pain is present, and having the information from the internal subconscious map, works to formulate an action plan. This all happens very quickly, in fact sometimes so quickly that waking consciousness is not even involved, and raw instinct dictates any action that is taken.

Emotional Pain and Identity

In Chapter 2, the subconscious is discussed as a repository for a model of the universe and archetypes or standards for the various ways a person engages the outside world.

In addition to the maps and archetypes, actual ego identities interact within those models. Each identity is shaped by models or ideals that are learned from experience and society. Each identity represents an aspect of who a person is, and having a secure sense of self is part of emotional health.

Emotional pain can occur when an identity model is attacked or challenged. For example, if a doctor performs a procedure that results in the death of a patient, an internal "good doctor" identity feels threatened, and the doctor experiences emotional pain. A good doctor feels compassion for the patient and the patient's family as well, but the identity of "good doctor" is challenged when losses are experienced.

Similarly, if a child is injured, a parent may experience emotional pain on multiple levels. At one level, a parent experiences empathetic pain. On another level, a parent's internal "good parent" identity experiences the pain of being challenged, thinking that he or she did not live up to the expectation of protecting the child from injury.

Guilt is the term often used to describe emotional pain resulting from not living up to an expectation or standard. Along with guilt, internal identities experience fear as well. A doctor who loses a patient also risks losing a license to practice, which would impact the doctor identity greatly. Similarly, an external agency judging a parent unfit could have devastating consequences to the parent identity. While guilt is a factor, other sources of emotional pain can be present as well. Emotional pain can be complicated.

Identities that develop during childhood can be a source of emotional pain as well. If a person has an embedded identity characteristic that believes "I am a failure," this person may avoid situations where success is even possible to avoid the pain of challenging the "failure" identity. Similarly, someone who has an identity that believes "I must always succeed" may avoid situations where perceived failure is possible. For example, rather than participating in a game or sport for fun or for the purpose of improving one's skills, a person may avoid games or sports altogether, or limit activities to a few that the person believes are always winnable.

Identities also exist at the deeper instinct / neurological level. These are protection identities. When a traumatic injury occurs, a protection identity remembers the detailed circumstances of the injury and warns the subconscious if those circumstances ever arise again.

For example, long after experiencing a car accident on a bridge, a person may try to avoid bridges while driving. If a bridge is encountered, the same feelings may occur as if the injury were recent, because an instinct level protection identity has the trauma imprinted on it. Post traumatic stress flash backs and dreams, for example, may be triggered by deep neurological memory, which may lay out an exact or exaggerated footprint of the universe at the time of the injury so that waking consciousness can formulate a plan to avoid the pain again. Without knowing the reason, waking consciousness may try to find alternative routes to lessen the threat that a bridge represents.

Spiritual Pain

When Spirituality is discussed, it is often in the context of existential realities. Human beings have a limited life span, and are separated from each other by physical bodies. One might say that human beings are ultimately alone and are going to die. To help mitigate these existential realities, the concept, hope, and idea that human consciousness exists outside the bounds of flesh and limited lifespan has been with humanity perhaps since the first incident of conscious awakening, and certainly from the beginnings of written language.

While death and being alone are part of the human condition, for most people they are at most background concerns. Exposure to death, trauma, and neglect can bring those concerns to the foreground, sometimes resulting in a deep-seated sense of dread. The symptoms of deep-seated dread may include emotional issues like depression and anxiety. The techniques presented in the practice at the end of this chapter can help address localized manifestations of the physical, emotional, and underlying spiritual pain. While the techniques presented here may be helpful, they are no substitute for professional help if emotional issues interfere with life and livelihood.

Eventually, everyone is confronted with existential realities, in aging, separation, and death. Since human instinct is specifically directed toward survival, the conflict that arises between instinct ego and existential realities can cause great distress, distracting a person from developing and sharing creative gifts.

Spirituality and faith are tools that can help a person to move forward in life and accept existential realities. The next chapter, which addresses faith and Spirituality directly, is geared toward moving through existential realities.

In summary, while physical pain may come from direct injury, emotional pain can rise from perceived challenge or injury against internal identities, and spiritual pain can result from consideration of existential realities and challenges. Within this program, the definition of physical and emotional pain is "response to actual or threat of damage to physical person or identity." Spiritual pain is defined as "a natural response to the existential realities of life that include mortality and physical separation."

Severity and Sensitivity

A person perceives and reacts to pain based on two factors. One factor is the severity of the threat or injury, and the other is the sensitivity or resilience of the person who experiences the threat or injury. Since everyone has different tolerance levels for pain, whether emotional (i.e. he has a "thin skin" and reacts to everything), or physical (i.e. she has a high tolerance for pain), the experience of pain is highly subjective. No one can interpret the pain level of another because every human being has unique experiences, circumstances, and neurology.

While stubbing a toe may be very painful for some people, a dancer or martial artist may initially experience a broken toe with hardly a notice, especially if the injury occurs in the middle of a performance or match. Conversely, while a glancing slap on the nose may go without notice to one person, a hypersensitive person, as illustrated in the "cowardly lion" character in the movie *The Wizard of Oz*, (Baum, 1939) may experience a level of pain that results in tears.

This is the reason that a medical or therapeutic professional asks a person to describe pain on a scale of 1 to 10. The experience of pain is subjective and depends on circumstance, memory, depth of injury, and neurological sensitivity.

Since neurology is associated with both physical and emotional pain, the effects of artificially introduced neurological agents including drugs and alcohol are worth discussing. Drugs and alcohol "work" by mimicking neurochemicals that the body produces naturally. Opioids, for example, mimic or look like endorphins to human neurology, and cannabis mimics endocannabinoids. Cocaine causes the body to be flooded with dopamine, while alcohol triggers dopamine and has a relaxing effect.

If a person experiences an injury, the body naturally produces endorphins to reduce the pain so that survival needs of fight or flight can be met. The addition of pain reducing medication reinforces the effects that the body produces naturally.

While medications may provide pain relief in short term situations, when taken over long periods of time they have the effect of altering a person's sensitivity. The way and degree to which these artificial agents alter sensitivity varies from person to person. For example, with prolonged the use of pain medications a person may become either more or less sensitive to pain. Over time, people develop an immunity to both the body's natural response and the artificial substance as well. Over time, more and more alcohol or pain medication will be required to experience the desired relief or effect.

Acute and Chronic Pain

Pain can be short term, or acute, as a direct reaction to an injury or perceived injury. For example, an employee who is chastised by a supervisor or manager may experience an acute feeling of emotional pain as his / her "good worker" identity is challenged. If the rebuke is small, job security is not threatened, and the employee's identity has adequate resilience, the effects of the rebuke is short lived. Acute pain, if not perceived as life or identity threatening, may simply require a physical or emotional bandage and soon may be forgotten.

On the other hand, if pain is recurring, or chronic, a simple bandage is not enough. For example, physically persistent pain might come from a known or unknown underlying condition, such as a back injury or a digestive system issue. Referring to the emotional pain example, the same rebuke from an employer experienced daily eventually will adversely affect an employee's performance and self-esteem. Emotionally persistent pain may manifest as feeling out of control or hopeless, which may produce anxiety or depression.

Spiritually and existentially, witnessing for example a cat killing a mouse may cause short term distress which, for most people, would pass relatively quickly. In this example, the impact would be acute assuming that no personal connection existed between the mouse and the witness. On the other hand, the loss of a loved one would produce a more persistent and chronic experience of loss. The loss would be experienced every time the loved one is absent from an activity that had been previously shared. This chronic experience of loss would likely result in an ongoing period of spiritual pain, manifested as grief.

Another word often associated with pain is suffering. Suffering may be defined as the energy a person adds to the experience of pain. For example, an injury or loss can be painful, but physical, emotional, and spiritual reaction to the injury or loss can result in suffering that lasts long after the initial effects (pain or shock) of the injury or loss fade away.

Suffering as Attachment

In a previous chapter the difference between healthy developmental attachment and unhealthy prolonged attachment is discussed. Prolonged emotional suffering may be considered a long-term unhealthy attachment. If a person becomes emotionally or spiritually attached to the memory of a painful incident, the suffering from that incident will persist. The attachment may manifest in fear, or avoidance, or in obsessive re-enactment to make sense of or control the pain or the incident. Unfortunately, a lot of painful circumstances happen for reasons that are well beyond any person's control, especially when the victims are children. Recurring cycles of suffering may develop with well-worn paths that seem to become a part of a person's existence. These recurring cycles may be considered "programmed reactions."

Programmed reactions become worn into the neurological pathways, creating a phenomenon called "the path to the well." To illustrate, one of the most basic human needs is for fresh water. Other than loss of oxygen, lack of fresh water will result in death sooner than almost anything else. At a deep neurological / instinctual level human instinct can memorize a pathway to a source for fresh water, so that even when not coherently conscious, a person may find a familiar fresh water source.

Like access to water, seeking out unhealthy relationships, behaviors, or substances that provide temporary relief from chronic pain also can be programmed into neurological memory. For example, when chronic physical or emotional pain is recognized, a person may seem to automatically reach for food, pornography, a drink or a pill, or an unhealthy relationship. The combination of "path to the well" programming, gradual desensitization to the effects of substances, and hypersensitization to external stimuli can all work together to form the trap of addiction.

Recovery from Painful Experience

In the introduction, a thesis that guides this program is presented. The thesis includes "developing and sharing creative gifts to the benefit of self and others." The experience of physical, emotional, and spiritual pain can have the effect of interrupting and redirecting creativity toward unhealthy and unproductive activities.

Ideally, after a person suffers a physical or emotional injury, there is a period of reduced activity while healing takes place. Eventually the human body and psyche find a "new normal" state. A good example of this reduced period of activity might be grieving the loss of a loved one, which has a huge impact on relational identity. While grieving can take years, and cannot be rushed, with the support of family, friends, and perhaps faith, identity adjustments occur eventually. When this happens "normal" creative activities can again produce a sense of joy and accomplishment, other relationships are experienced with joy and comfort, and life goes on.

In discussing severity of pain and sensitivity to pain, the effect substances have on the body's ability to manage pain and healing was described. Chronic use of addictive external substances and chronic behaviors can interfere with the human body, mind, and spirit's normal resilience. A person's ability to exercise creativity and experience joy is disrupted by an obsessive seeking behavior. Eventually all creativity is focused on obtaining and using whatever substance or habit with which a person is obsessed. Relationships are disrupted because they no longer produce comfort and joy. Neuroreceptors are overwhelmed by the flood of substance or habitual experience, and the body loses its ability to respond to naturally occurring neurochemicals. Naturally produced dopamine is no longer adequate for experiencing creativity and joy; oxytocin no longer adequate for relationships; serotonin does not provide a sense of relaxation and well-being; and naturally occurring endorphins no longer produce pleasure and relief from pain. Even naturally occurring endocannabinoids no longer spur creative imagination. Life is disrupted.

Spiritual Energy and Pain: The Eastern Model

The internal energy model presented in the last chapter recognizes energy centers, or chakras, and the energy flow that emanates from those chakras. Chakra energy flows through the body in much the same fashion as blood, oxygen, nourishment, and neurochemicals flow. In the Eastern model, rather than viewing injury as an area in the body from which pain emanates, injury is understood as an area in the body where healing energies are blocked from flowing. The concept is not so foreign to Western medicine. For example, an injury that results in blockage of blood flow will result in deprivation of oxygen and nutrients to the affected area, causing pain. If the injured area is not attended, more severe long-term complications can occur. Similarly, the blockage of Spiritual energy flow can also cause both acute pain and prolonged suffering.

In Western medicine, there are predominantly two responses to injury or pain – medicate and / or operate. To be fair, taking time to heal coupled with appropriate physical therapy activities are also often prescribed. But in the West, little attention is paid to energy flows. To some people, attending to energy flow may sound strange, but there are many practical applications for this approach to pain and healing. Practices like acupuncture and reiki, as well as some holistic orthopedic practices help many people every day. Many of these practices are founded on the idea of opening blockages to the free flow of healing energy.

The practice associated with pain mitigation and healing has already been explored to some extent. The visualization of chakra energy centers and release of negative energy is a form of this practice. However, instead of focusing on the chakras which are the source of energy flows, this pain mitigation practice focuses on unblocking specific areas of pain. In his book "Dissolving Pain," Les Fehmi describes a similar technique for resolving pain based on his work in biofeedback. (Fehmi & Robbins, 2007)

Exercise: Identifying Areas of Recurring Pain

The exercise begins by identifying areas in your body where physical pain occurs on a repeated basis. Everyone gets occasional headaches, and many people have areas where injuries have occurred and pain is experienced in the location of the injuries. As people get older, chronic issues like weather related arthritis pain may occur in specific areas of the body. Consider areas where physical pain occurs, and assign a number between 1 and 10 to the intensity of a typical pain experience. For example, a person might identify occasional headaches that rise to a level of 2, which is simply an annoyance. A person might also identify pain resulting from a knee injury that rises to a level of 6 when the weather changes.

While physical pain, such as back pain, joint pain, or even headache pain is relatively easy to locate in the body, emotional pain is more subtle. A moment of reflection can usually reveal areas in the body where emotional distress manifests. For example, for some people, anxiety may feel like a lump in the throat or tension behind the eyes. Depression may feel like a sinking feeling in the gut or a dull thud in the back of the head. Fear may feel like tension in the shoulders or tightness in the lower back. Anger or resentment may feel like heated ears or tightness in the chest. Consider areas of the body where emotional pain manifests and assign a level of 1 to 10 to the intensity of the experience. In this case, if anxiety that occurs with a "lump in throat" feeling rises to a level that is debilitating and results in a person self isolating or cancelling plans to socialize, the emotional pain level may be a 10.

Spiritual pain also has physical manifestations, and may be hard to differentiate from emotional pain. A deep-seated sense of "not being safe" may also feel like anxiety, accompanied by a knot in the stomach or lump in the throat. A deep-seated sense of loneliness may feel like depression and manifest in an emptiness in the chest, for example. Once again, assigning a 1 to 10 level helps quantify the experience.

For the exercise, create a written list that contains the top two or three sources of physical, emotional, and spiritual pain you may have experienced. Record the physical location in your body associated with the pain, and the intensity that the pain rises to, from 1 to 10.

Practice Benefits and Challenges:

In addition to the immediate sensation of physical or emotional pain, a sense of being "not in control" adds a dimension of fear which increases suffering. Consciously locating physical or emotional pain in the body helps to objectify the pain. Objectifying the pain makes the pain a finite quantity, which helps a person to feel more in control and makes the pain easier to manage. Feeling a little more in control can help a person relax, which can also provide some measure of relief.

After an area of pain is physically located, the practice of visualizing the energy blockage being swept away can begin. The practice allows a person to feel as if she / he is actively participating in the removal of pain, which also helps a person to feel more in control.

In early Western medicine, bodily fluids known as "humours" were thought to flow through a healthy body. The early western analog to holistic spiritually aware practices were thought to restore the natural flow of healing "humours." In this case the humours in question include neurochemicals, hormones, antibodies, and all the wonderful proteins, amino acids, and other substances the human body produces naturally. In a real sense, healing happens when blockages are opened and flow of natural energies and humours is restored.

In practice, over 90% of the people taught these techniques recognize benefit (*Authors Note: This is an observation from working as a Spiritual Director in an addiction detox program, not based on statistical data). After completing the practice, most say their pain is reduced by a point or two on a scale of 1 to 10. Others say whatever pain they experienced has been completely alleviated. For a few people, the practice of visualizing the area of pain increases the feeling of pain. If this practice has the effect of increasing rather than alleviating pain, return to the practice of diaphragm breathing which also promotes relaxation and healing.

None of the practices presented in this program are substitutes for licensed medical and therapeutic help. Underlying conditions can be quite serious and deserve proper medical and psychotherapeutic attention. This practice is one option of many to help alleviate suffering. And just as underlying physical conditions can be serious and require proper diagnoses and treatment, underlying mental health issues such as depression and addiction can be dangerous, and can lead to death without proper treatment. This practice is meant to supplement medical and therapeutic support and help to alleviate pain and suffering. There are no promises of "miraculous cure" in this or any of these practices.

Practice:

As described in the exercise, begin by noting areas in your body where you experience physical pain. For this practice, choose an area that you think has the highest priority. Now, on a scale of 1 to 10, make a note of how intense the pain is.

Next, note any emotional pain you are experiencing. Note the location in your body where the emotional pain is most prevalent. Do your emotions come with the feeling of a lump in your throat? A lump in your stomach? Tightness in the shoulders? Pain behind the eyes? Wherever that pain is located, note it, and note how intense you think that emotional pain is on a scale of 1 to 10, where 1 is hardly noticeable and 10 is hardly bearable.

Sitting in a relaxed and upright posture, begin to center yourself and focus on breathing from your diaphragm. Also, remember to associate your breathing with a safe space. If during this or any practice you experience any distress, you can always return your attention to your breathing.

Breathing with your diaphragm, be conscious of your stomach moving. Notice any external distractions in your environment. Fans blowing, family members moving about, and outside traffic noise are things you cannot control. One by one, recognize, accept, and let go of the distractions, and continue to breathe.

After letting go of external distractions, notice the physical distractions that your body produces. Little tickles, itches, and a desire to cough may arise. As your body relaxes, these sensations are natural. Recognize distractions one by one and adjust yourself for comfort. Cough if you need to, scratch where it itches, and return your attention to your breathing. As always, the number one rule is kindness to self. You are not trying to control anything, you are just breathing, recognizing, and accepting.

After attending to physical distractions, notice random thoughts and feelings moving through your brain. Thoughts are also normal. Just as you did with the external and physical distractions, accept the thoughts and feelings one by one and continue to breathe.

After a few minutes of relaxed breathing and letting go of distractions, bring your attention to the area in your body where you experience or have experienced physical pain. Can you visualize the area of pain? Can you recognize the intensity of the pain?

Now try to visualize the intensity of the pain using color. If the pain is very intense, you may visualize the area as being red. As you visualize that area of pain, continue to recognize your breathing. Imagine that every inhale sweeps in to that area and brings healing energy. With every exhale, imagine the intensity of the pain dissipating. Each breath reduces any blockage to energy flow, allowing the breath energy to sweep through. Repeat this process for several minutes. Imagine that inhaling brings healing energy, and exhaling dissipates pain intensity.

You may notice the intensity of the pain diminishing, reducing with every exhale. The area of pain may move from a color of red to orange. Cooling, healing energy continues to flow. With every exhale, the pain dissipates. If the pain is not dissipating, no worries, just continue to breathe. Breath energy alone can bring relaxation which helps dissipate pain. If the breathing seems comfortable and helpful, and if the pain has diminished, imagine the orange pain level cooling to yellow. Continue breathing. As you continue, yellow may reduce to green, and finally, when the pain dissipates completely, the area of pain changes from green to blue.

Now move your attention to an area of emotional pain. Can you visualize the area of the pain? Can you recognize the intensity of it? Can you visualize the natural chakra energies trying to flow through this area? Can you sense the blockage to healing energy flow? This time, visualize the area of pain being very dark. As you inhale, you may notice some light starting to open the area of blockage. Darkness cannot abide in the light. With every inhale, the light warms and relaxes the area of darkness. With every exhale, the darkness dissipates. Like knots being loosened, the area of emotional pain relaxes. Every inhale brings light and warmth. With every exhale the cold darkness dissipates. Almost as if the sun is rising on this area of pain, warmth and relaxation increases.

If the pain persists, no worries. Just continue to breathe. Every breath relaxes your whole body. Your safe space is within your grasp, easily accessed. If the pain seems to dissipate, continue to breathe, continue to bring in the light. Continue to exhale that area of darkness away.

Once emotional pain has been attended, visualize your entire body. Visualize every inhale sweeping through your entire body. With every breath, little areas of tension are relaxed, little areas of darkness are warmed with light. With your blood flow, every breath you take literally touches every cell in your body, from the top of the head, to the tip of every toe, to every fingertip. Every inhale brings healing; and every exhale releases darkness. Imagine the energy circulating like a warm light throughout your entire body. Smile.

Now allow yourself to feel positive regard for yourself. Gratitude abounds. Think of the immediate area around you. Think of people and even pets in your home; think of fellow meditators if you are in a group. Allow your inner light to expand to them, feeling positive regard and gratitude. Expand your area of perception to include your neighbors and your local town. Include all the creatures in the parks and forests, including plants and animals and fish in the lakes and brooks. Expand outward to include your state or province, and then expand further to include the country in which you are residing. Breathe in the light on behalf of all, and radiate warmth and gratitude toward all. Now, expand your perception to include the entire world. Inhale the light; exhale healing, positive regard, and gratitude.

Now open your eyes. Congratulations. You have completed the

pain mitigation meditation exercise.

Take a moment to consider the pain levels you noted prior to the practice. How do the pain levels compare? If you had a physical pain area with a severity of 8, has it reduced to a level of 6 or lower? How about emotional pain? Has that lump in your throat dissipated? Is the heaviness in your chest lighter?

This is part of the author's daily practice. At the age of 60+, depending on the weather, I have some arthritis pain in my hands and shoulders. I have areas in my body where there are chronic concerns, including my heart, cholesterol, and other long-term injuries. (Note: While I include my cholesterol levels in my meditation, I also monitor my cholesterol with my doctor. This practice is not a substitute for professional care.)

And, like many people, I suffer from occasional anxiety which usually manifests as heaviness in my chest or a sinking feeling in my gut. Sometime, when I get a headache or when the anxiety springs up during the day, I engage in this practice spontaneously. With practice my "path to the well" has come to include focusing on areas of pain and "breathing through them."

Many women engage in focused breathing automatically as well when suffering pain or injury. For many, Lamaze training and giving birth to children imprint this reaction into neural memory.

For most people, this practice provides some relief from pain, even if temporarily. Use this as often as you need, and share it with other people who are receptive.

5 HIGHER POWER AS OTHER

In the last chapter, physical, emotional, and spiritual pain are discussed. Characteristics of pain are discussed, including sensitivity, resilience, and acute vs chronic pain. The connection between suffering and attachment is discussed, and a spiritual model is introduced that connects pain with the blockage of spiritual energy flow. The practice provides meditation tools for releasing blockages to energy flow that cause pain.

In this chapter, the concept of "God as Other" is introduced. Characteristics of Spirit are explored, including life, consciousness, and male and female aspects. Evolution is explored as a way to understand Spirit, and Spirit is described in terms of Transcendence, Grace, and Diversity.

Narrative:

It was a lovely spring Sunday morning; the new leaves on the trees glowed with chartreuse tenderness. Birds called with a renewed sense of joy and vigor; the last vestiges of snow having disappeared from the roadsides. Alone in the car, driving home from a Palm Sunday Christian service, the young man spontaneously asked a question out loud. "God, are there trees and birds in heaven?"

He was surprised to receive an immediate response. Not in voice, but in a feeling of overwhelming peace and affirmation. "Yes, there are trees and birds in heaven."

Surprised, the young man continued his query: "In heaven, will I be able to learn and grow as a person?"

"Yes, you will continue to learn and grow as a person."

"Is there anything I can do in this life that I will not be able to do in an

54

afterlife?"

"In the afterlife, there is no suffering nor death. In this life, you have the opportunity to help people who experience suffering and loss."

Tearing up with emotion, the young man knew he had received his calling. His life would be shaped from that moment on by this experience.

Divine Other

Thus far, the focus of this practice has been on self. Both the consciousness model and the sacred energy model focus on mindful awareness of self. Focus on self is both powerful and insufficient. In fact, it might be said that the greatest weakness of mindfulness and meditation practice is the sole focus on self. If a person's only reference is self, how is a person to learn and grow? Internal awareness is powerful and necessary, but self-awareness is not sufficient for creative development.

Humans are social beings. People develop with care and guidance from parents, from teachers, and from interaction with peers. People also develop through interaction with the external universe, including people, books, and interaction with culture and ethnicity.

In a later chapter, healthy relationships and reaching outside of self to connect with others is explored. For this chapter, Divine Other will be explored, Other with a capital "O."

People view and connect with Divinity in a variety of ways. Many people connect with Divinity through ethnic, cultural, and religious affiliations. Christians, Jews, Muslims, Buddhists, Hindus, and others all have developed wonderful traditions describing and connecting with Divine Other.

To consider Divine Other, recall the consciousness model from previous chapters. Remember that the model includes layers of consciousness and a Sacred Core. Horizontally, the model is confined to the interior, with a skin boundary. Outside of the skin boundary lies the external physical universe, including relationships.

In the model, the Sacred Core runs vertically, and consists of energy centers or chakras. But what is outside the sacred energy core? Is there a source of Divine Energy outside of the internal chakra energy sources?

While the physical universe may be considered immanent or within the grasp of humanity, the external Source of Divine energy may be considered Transcendent or beyond the physical grasp of humanity.

Judeo-Christian-Islamic traditions suggest a model where transcendent Divine Other is somehow above humanity, and death (or worse, damnation) is located below humanity. This association with heaven as source of life and earth as place of death or damnation has been engraved culturally in the hearts and minds of many people. From this cultural perspective, the idea of Transcendence above and immanence below seems natural, as when life leaves the body the decaying remnants return to the earth. "Ashes to ashes, dust to dust."

Associating damnation with the earth hardly seems fair, however, as life springs forth from the earth as well. Many worldwide traditions, including pre-Hebrew traditions, recognize the earth from the perspective of fertility, as the source of life. After all, water, minerals, and plants spring forth from the earth, providing energy and sustenance to animal and human life.

Thinking of earth as a source of life may challenge monotheistic Judeo-Christian-Islamic traditionalists. After all, earth-based life-giving deities were set aside long ago. Or were they? Even in Judaic tradition, Spirit is acknowledged in terms of both breath Spirit, or life itself, and thought, or Consciousness Spirit. Life Spirit is described using words like Ruach in Hebrew, Pneuma in Greek, and Prana in Sanskrit. Consciousness Spirit is described using words like Nephesh from Hebrew, Psyche from Greek, and Chitta from Sanskrit. Both breath/life and consciousness are constituent parts of all living creatures.

Monotheists believe thought and life energy originate from one source, namely God. Hinduism recognizes Transcendent Other in many different manifestations. Trinitarian thought (both Christian and Buddhist) recognizes Transcendent Other in three facets or aspects. Even Islamic theology recognizes one God manifesting from as many as 99 different perspectives or "names."

Nondual Divinity

In monotheistic traditions, the word or name God represents Divine Other. In Monotheistic traditions, God is the source of both life and consciousness; God has attributes of immanence and transcendence; and humanity made in the image of God is both male and female. God is one, and God has many aspects or attributes.

Western thought attempts to describe Transcendence in dualistic terms, for example good vs evil, light vs dark, and life vs death. Eastern Monistic traditions consider all dualistic differentiations mere illusions. The differences between self and other, between God and humanity, and between God and creation are all illusions; all things are one.

In contrast, the nondual perspective recognizes the possibility of both unity and difference. From the nondual perspective, God is One and God has multiple aspects and attributes. Self and other are both connected and individual beings. All things are connected and diverse at the same time.

God as transcendent Divine Other can also be understood as Transcendent Spirit. The nondual aspects of Spirit, Breath and Consciousness, may be interpreted in terms of female and male. As giver of life / breath and source of sustenance and nurture, God may be associated with female attributes. As giver of conscious thought, God may be associated with male attributes.

This is not to say that attributes of life and conscious thought are strictly male or female. These associations are simply consistent with many traditions, not as an endorsement of stereotypes.

Divine Other as Male and Female

Understanding God in terms of both male and female aspects is useful for many reasons. The interpretation that God is male has been used to subjugate and deny women and girls basic human rights for much of human history. Shamefully, Judeo-Christian traditions have used the idea of Divine Transcendence to justify the treatment of women as property throughout history. And while Islam generally regards women as autonomous beings, their rights are severely restricted in many Islamic cultures.

For some people, relating to a Divine Other with male attributes is difficult or even impossible. Trauma in the form of abuse or neglect at the hands of a male family member, sexual identity related challenges, or just a sense of "not being able to relate" creates barriers between many people and male transcendent Divine Other. Some people just have a natural tendency to relate to a Grounded Mother figure rather than Transcendent Father.

On the other hand, thousands of years of "God as male" tradition creates a barrier to accepting Transcendent Other in female terms. In Judaic tradition, female Deity was banished with the Canaanite

Goddess (or Yahwist consort) Asherah. However, even in the Jewish tradition there is a female voice representing Transcendence. In the Judaic book of Proverbs, the Wisdom of God, which is "Sophia" in Greek, is portrayed using female pronouns. Proverbs 1:20-21 says that "Wisdom cries aloud in the streets, raises her voice in the squares. [21] At the head of the busy streets she calls; at the entrance of the gates, in the city, she speaks out;" (Tanakh, 1985) Similarly, in Christianity, Mary as mother of Jesus is often associated with Divinity as well, especially in Catholicism.

While traditional names used to represent Divine Transcendence are usually interpreted as male, "Mary Sophia" is an alternative name to consider for representing the Divine Female aspect of transcendent Divine Other.

In one of the Judaic creation accounts shared by Christianity and Islam, God breathed the breath of life, "Ruach" into the Earth, and a new and unique living human soul rose up from the dust. The female breath / life aspect of God is often associated with the earth from which life and sustenance spring forth.

In the same creation account, the gift of Ruach yields conscious life, "Nephesh." Nephesh consciousness animates life and allows movement and communication. God as pure conscious thought spoke words which brought forth creation and life. God as conscious thought became associated with heaven or sky above the earth. The tradition of communicating with male God "in heaven" through conscious prayer continues today.

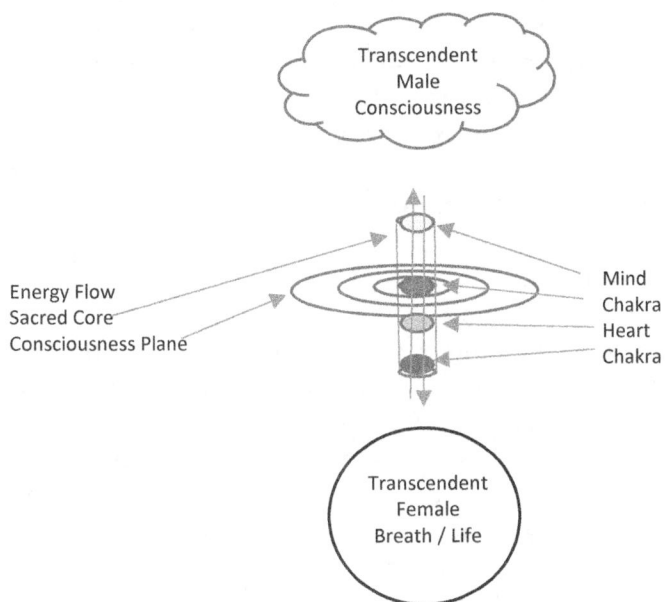

Figure 6: Transcendent Male and Female

Divine Other in Consciousness Model

The understanding of transcendent Divine Other in terms of nondual "Sky Father" and "Earth Mother" is useful for this LLCA model of consciousness. Within the sacred core, Divine Consciousness Energy flows between Sky and Earth, while Divine Life energy flows between Earth and Sky. The Divine Energy flows create and fuel internal chakras with life and consciousness energy. Sky and Earth are separate and Other, and creation and humanity exist because of the creative flow of energy between Transcendent Sky Consciousness and Earth Life / Breath Spirit.

In Christian Trinitarian theology God is Three distinct beings, and God is also One. From the LLCA perspective, the Sky-Earth model includes Transcendent Sky Father, Immanent Earth Mother, and Holy Spirit Relationship flowing through humanity and bringing the gifts of life and consciousness. From the Judaic scripture perspective, one might visualize Ruach Spirit bringing forth life, and Nephesh Spirit giving life the conscious capacity to sustain itself. Male and female energies are also described in Tantric Buddhist Philosophy, flowing through male and female energy channels. (Yeshe, 2001)

The Divine Energy flow model of life and creation that originated in longstanding traditions and cultures can also be discerned within in the cosmological development of the universe and life.

Evolutionary Development

Beginning with the "Big Bang," plasma energy cooled into gases which coalesced into stars. Stars exploded and formed other stars, which generated more complex elements like oxygen, carbon, and iron. The earth (and presumably similar planets) eventually formed with liquid water, atmosphere, and blue skies.

Over time, complex proteins developed and formed rudimentary building blocks of life, eventually forming primitive viruses and single celled creatures. Cells replicated and specialized, and creatures emerged including plants, fish, reptiles, birds, and eventually mammals, rodents, apes, and humans.

Lifeless matter and energy follow predictable patterns, obedient to the laws of physics. When the breath of life and consciousness was introduced, life began to take its own course. Attracted to light and nutrients, repulsed by harsh environments, life defied the laws of physics and began to plot its own course. Survival became the driving instinct of consciousness.

Eventually the drive to survive expanded to include nurture, cooperation, and love. For example, reptiles drop and abandon their eggs and the young must survive using instincts. Birds provide more care for their young, and with evolution, mammals care for their young for longer and longer periods of time. Communities of flocks and herds form, as do lifelong intimate relationships in some species. Within humanity, children are raised and nurtured through young adulthood, and communities are formed.

From a Spiritual perspective, it is possible to interpret the evolution of life toward greater compassion, greater love, and greater community as "Divine DNA" guiding the development of life. Human care of the earth's ecology indicates that the concept of "community" is expanding to include all life, the entire planet, and the entire Cosmos.

But evolution toward inclusive love and community is not

complete, as conflict also plays a major role in human history. Earliest recorded history describes the formation of family-oriented tribes, which formed nations, which developed ever advancing technologies for the purposes of conquest and defense. Early warlords fashioned their gods in each their own likeness and image, each claiming the prime lineage of godhood to justify wars and the dehumanization, conquering, and enslavement of neighbors near and far.

In contrast to wars, some nations found common causes and formed alliances. Civilizations separated by oceans and mountains came into dialog. Dialog revealed that despite the differences of race, ethnicity, and culture, humanity has much in common in seeking and relating to Transcendent Spirit.

Transcendent Commonalities

Buddhist contemplative practices which have origins in Hinduism, have much in common with Jewish Kabbalah, Sikh, and Christian contemplative practices, as well as mystical Islamic practices. Sacred writings from all cultures contain instructions to treat others with kindness and respect, to love one another, and to trust in the presence and power of unconditional love. In Hinduism and Buddhism, unconditional love and justice are expressed as "Dharma," in Islam "Ar-Rahim," in Judaism "Chesed," and in Christianity "Grace."

Humanity has such a wonderful heritage of religions, cultures, and philosophies to draw upon. Earth centered Pagan and Wiccan cultures evolve into love centered cultures, and many native and Shamanic cultures have preserved much in the way of love centered wisdom. Old prejudices have begun to drop away; harmonies between cultures are recognized, and differences are celebrated rather than feared and challenged. Women and people of differing sexual orientations who had been excluded and oppressed and persecuted throughout recorded history are finally being accepted, empowered, loved, and celebrated.

Whereas cosmological and biological evolution suggest a "Female / Ruach / Divine DNA" development toward compassion, love, and community, cultural evolution suggests a "Male / Nephesh" consciousness evolution toward the same. This bears repeating: both biological and conscious evolutionary paths indicate a movement toward compassion, love, and community.

There is hope in recognizing that at broad macro evolutionary and societal levels, life is evolving toward community and love.

Transcendent Differences

Within the evolving community of humanity, individuals search for meaning and purpose. People seek connection with transcendent meaning that goes beyond self. People look externally to religions and cultures, to philosophers and priests, and find concepts that resonate with their own individual experiences of meaning and Transcendence. Sometimes people experience internal ecstatic inspiration from what appears to be Divine Other, which can inspires loving service.

Just as tribal ancestors imagined heroes and gods that were formed in their image, individual people continue to do much the same today. While broad conceptional icons of Transcendent Deity exist within larger cultural contexts, smaller communities and individuals imagine and experience Transcendent Deity in ways that align much more closely to individual experiences. For example, the Jesus of ancient Jewish heritage bears little resemblance to the Jesus of modern Christianity. Even within Christianity, the Protestant Evangelical Jesus looks very different from the Catholic, the Eastern Orthodox, or the Progressive Jesus. And within each of these Christian subcontexts, individuals imagine and experience Jesus in individualized ways. While Jewish scripture says God created humanity in God's image, humans do much to form God in the image of humans.

When a human approaches the Divine with imagination, the context that the imagination uses is limited to his or her own experience. The limitation of imagination to one's own context and experience is part of the human condition. Remarkably, for some who seek Transcendence, Transcendence sometimes reaches back and inspires understanding quite beyond the limitations of experience. And the experience of "Divine Inspiration" happens within all traditions, including Hindu, Buddhist, Christian, Muslim, Jewish, Pagan, etc. Transcendent Divine Other reaches from eternity, beyond time and space, into the bounded temporal finitude of creation. Experience of Transcendence results in awe and inspiration. When such inspiration occurs, the common message both encoded into human evolution and received through Transcendent inspiration is unconditional love.

In Judaic scripture there is a story of a time when all of humanity spoke the same language and came together to build a great tower, the Tower of Babel. As the story goes, God confounded the language of humanity as a curse. The building project was abandoned, and humanity scattered and formed diverse languages and cultures. (Tanakh, 1985. Gen 11:1-9) But one may ask, does that story represent a curse or a gift? If one believes in unconditionally loving Divine Other, one must consider the possibility that this act of creating diversity was actually a gift.

From the perspective of creativity, diversity is most obviously a gift. Building a bridge that will stand the test of time requires many disciplines, including geology, artistry, engineering, and labor. Building a society requires healers, builders, farmers, and inspired leaders. Diversity is a valuable gift for humanity.

The vast diversity of culture, ethnicity, and creative gifts inspires the many diverse interpretations of transcendent Divine Other. And as diverse, beloved, creative beings, every individual also has unique experiences and insights into the nature of Transcendent Spirit as Other.

Most cultures and religions believe their interpretation of Transcendence is authentic and exclusive, and warn that attempting to explore other understandings can lead to tragedy if not to eternal damnation. Allah is the only God. Jesus is the only path to the Father. Jewish scripture says "Hear now Oh Israel, our God is One" (Tanakh, 1985. Deut. 6:4).

By contrast, Hinduism has many manifestations of God to consider, from the elephant headed child Ganesh to the furious and frightening Kali. And although there are theistic traditions within Buddhism, Buddhism is also considered a non-theistic philosophy that illuminates the path to enlightenment. With all these voices from cultures, religions, and the human tendency to shape God in each our own images, how does one discern authentic Transcendence?

The observation that life and consciousness are evolving in the direction of unconditional love suggests that the presence of love and the absence of hate are characteristics of authentic Transcendent Divine Other. In Christian scripture, Paul speaks of "knowing a tree by the fruit it bears" (NRSV, 1989. Gal 5:22). If a manifestation of Transcendent Divine inspires love, peace, patience, kindness, gentleness, faithfulness, generosity, and self-control, the inspiration is authentic. Buddhist Dharma, Islamic Ar Rahim, Jewish Chesed, and Christian Grace all suggest that unconditional love reveals Authentic Spirit.

Exercise Spiritual Self Awareness:

With the idea of Authentic Transcendent Spirit in mind, consider the following exercise as a way of further building self-awareness. Past exercises discuss identity in terms of culture, gifts, and relationships. The purpose of this exercise is to develop a sense of Spiritual Identity.

Some of the concepts described earlier are included in the exercise, like affinity toward earth / sky, and female / male attributes of Divinity. Earth centered people tend to relate better with animals and nature than with people. They tend to enjoy communing with nature, and they tend to enjoy earth related activities like gardening and hiking. Earth centered people are often the voices calling attention to ecological issues like global warming. Earth centered people mourn when the earth is hurt from ecological disasters like reactor melt downs, oil spills, and when great glaciers break away from land and melt into oceans.

Sky-oriented people tend to be dreamers and thinkers, dedicating more time to exploration of ideas and concepts than studying natural phenomena. Reading and creative expression of ideas tend to occupy the time of sky centered people.

For this exercise, take some time to answer the following questions:

- Do you feel more connected with Grounded Earth or Transcendent Sky concepts and activities? To what extent are you drawn toward either perspective?

- Are you drawn toward Internal or External Expression of Faith? (i.e. church and community work vs internal practices like prayer and meditation. To what extent?)

- Are you more comfortable with female or male expressions of Divinity? To what extent?

- How do the messages of your origin religion and culture inspire you?

- What concepts or messages within your religion or culture challenge you?

- Do any cultures and religions outside of your culture of origin seem interesting or worthy of exploration and understanding? Which ones and why?

- How has Unconditional Love manifested in your life, your relationships, and your work?

Practice Preparation:

Before moving into the practice, consider earlier discussions regarding human development. Remember that people who form secure attachments when very young are more likely to develop and mature into healthy and productive adults. When a baby forms secure attachments with parents, she or he feels secure in being curious and in exploring and learning about the surrounding world. The child will play with other children and form relationships outside the parent-child bond. Over time children develop stronger relationships outside the parent bond, with the potential of eventually forming intimate relationships.

While childhood secure attachment may be ideal, the fact is that no childhood is ideal. Loss, and neglectful and abusive experiences are also part of the human experience. Without the solid foundation of secure attachment, children may experience difficulties in development and in forming healthy relationship bonds. Even the best parents need to make a living and take time for self-care, and challenges occur in the best of childhoods. Families move away from childhood friends and security, and tragic losses can occur when a child is young.

But all is not lost. Relationship with "God as Other" can do more than inspire and guide creative development. A solid relationship with "God as Other" can help fill in "secure attachment gaps" that may have developed during childhood.

Divine Communion practice is based on the Tantric "Guru Yoga" practice. Guru Yoga is intended to use meditation to increase Spiritual connection with living or deceased teachers or gurus. In this LLCA practice, connection with Divine Transcendent Love will be explored.

Assuming this practice somehow conjures or invokes communion with Divine Spirit would be quite arrogant. While controlling Transcendent Other is neither reasonable nor possible, inviting Divine Spirit to connect and dwell within is possible. The assumption that Unconditionally Loving Spirit responds positively to such an invitation is also reasonable. A relationship with Spirit based on invitation and loving response inspires humility, respect, gratitude, and love.

Practice: Divine Communion

For this practice, begin as always with a comfortable upright posture and intentional breathing from the diaphragm. Remember that breath is the focal point and safe space. When internal or external distractions arise, accept the distraction and return attention to your breathing. Given your experience with previous practices, let go of distractions should be getting easier. Recognize, accept, and letting go of external distractions. Then consciously recognize, accept, and release distracting internal thoughts and feelings.

From the breathing practice, move into recognizing and releasing consciousness layers one by one. First release conscious thoughts, then move inward and let go of subconscious identities and feelings. Move inward again and accept and let go of instinctual "fight or flight" urges that may come into your awareness. Moving past the wall of instinctual urges, take a moment to breathe in the Sacred Breeze within your Divine Core.

Once comfortably centered in the Divine Core, recognize your mind, heart, core, and root chakras. One by one, let your breath energy sweep in and cleanse out distractions within your mind, attachments and resentments within your heart, fears within your core, and obsessions and any residual guilt or shame within your root. Recognize being in a place of complete emptiness, and take a moment to breathe and rest. Remember that emptiness is a space of observing without filter, being fully present and transparent, as if light and air can pass right through you.

If any physical or emotional discomforts are present, take a moment to visualize and release them one by one. Once comfortable, relaxed, and sufficiently empty, move into the Divine Communion practice.

Take a moment to open your senses to your Higher Power. Whether your Higher Power is manifest in Jesus, Mary Sophia, Spirit, God as Father, God as Mother, or some other unconditional loving presence, try to imagine the Presence of the Higher Power you would invite into communion. Sometimes this can be very difficult; if a visualization or feeling is not apparent, do not be discouraged. Assume that Spirit is present.

Divine Presence can be startling. If you are startled and want to break from the practice or if you want to continue, either way is fine. Remember, the number one rule is to be kind to yourself.

If you can, imagine the touch of Divine Presence. Sometimes a person may sense Divine Presence close at hand, like a reassuring hug. Remember how important face and touch can be during development; this connection with Divinity can help provide a sense of comfort and fulfillment. You are not alone. You are loved. Transcendent Unconditional Love abides within. Divine Presence is not controlling, just present and inspiring.

The next step of the process is to invite Transcendence into your mind chakra. Where once there was confusion, invite in peace and clarity. As you inhale, you may imagine the breath of Divine Presence entering your body, filling the space that was emptied. You may sense a general feeling of well-being as Divine Presence communes with your mind. Some people drift off to sleep during this portion of the practice, while others may experience waking dream visions. The mind chakra is a center of creativity, and Divine Other is often a powerful source of creativity. While creative experiences are informative and contribute to mindfulness, try to avoid distraction from the direct experience of peace and clarity. Creative expression is present and will remain so, but for now allow peace and clarity to develop. Every inhale invites in open-minded peace and clarity. Every exhale allows the dissipation of confusion and chaos.

You may dwell in this peaceful place of mind-communion for several minutes.

Next, move your attention to your heart. With resentments and attachments cleaned out, there is now space for love. Love of self, love of other, love that is without condition. As you inhale, allow yourself to invite Divine Love to fill your heart.

The human heart is fragile and often accumulates scar tissue from experiences over time. Imagine Divine Love gently massaging, softening, and healing any scar tissue. Allow the open space of your heart to fill to the point of overflowing. Allow Love to spill through the rest of your body. Sharing this love with others will be explored during the relationship practice, but for now allow yourself to experience this Healing Grace for yourself. You are a beloved being made in the Image of God. You are allowed to accept love, and in so doing to recognize your worthiness for being loved. Transcendent Grace is unconditional. You are loved.

After several minutes of experiencing Divine Love in your heart, turn your attention to your core chakra area. Having emptied the core of fears and burdens, space is available for faith. Faith includes faith in self, Faith in Higher Power, and the self confidence that comes with faith. Recognize that you are not alone; an Advocate abides, providing encouragement and support.

Faith tends to be interpreted as a future oriented gift. For this exercise, faith is not about what is coming, but rather faith is oriented toward the here and now. Faith describes your ability to handle whatever life brings.

Another characteristic that grows within the core chakra is Wisdom. Wisdom comes with experience, including both successes and failures. According to Jewish Scripture, Wisdom is the specifically female manifestation of Divinity. Wisdom understands that hardships and challenges pass with time. Wisdom grows hand in hand with faith. While faith carries hope and strength, wisdom carries confidence and peace. For women, the core is located near the location of the womb, where the ultimate creative act of growing new life takes place. Divine Other inspires creativity here as well.

Dwell in your core chakra for several minutes, experiencing the inspiration of Faith, Serenity, and Wisdom. When ready, move attention to your root chakra.

Recall that the space where the root chakra is located is a center of creative passion and joy. Inviting Divine Other to connect with your root chakra may inspire bursts of passion and energy. Joy comes with the spark of creation, with the breathing of life into the earth and forming new, creative consciousness. Passion for life, passion for love, and passion for creative gifts may emerge, along with the pure joy one might experience in a loving embrace. In this space, the kind of near ecstasy written about by prophets and dreamers is accessible. This is not the temporary kind of ecstasy that might be induced with external stimulation. This ecstasy comes in holistic harmony with the energy within all chakras. Hope, faith, love, clarity, peace, and wisdom are also present. This ecstasy is not an end unto itself; it is rather part of something much greater than the individual pieces. This ecstasy, this joy, this creative passion, is real and sustainable, generative, and not consuming.

You may dwell in this place of joyful communion for several minutes. Then, with gratitude, return attention to your breathing. You are grounded. You are connected. You are beloved. And you are whole. Imagine Divine Communion Energy filling your body.

Like all practices, this one closes with a sense of humility and gratitude. Allow positive intentions toward self and positive intentions toward others. Allow positive intensions toward family, friends, and neighbors. Allow positive intentions towards other living creatures and plants. Widening your attention, allow positive intentions toward others in your local town, your state or province, and widen out to include positive intentions toward your nation of residence. Finally, allow your positive intentions to extend outward to include everyone in the world.

With a cleansing breath, allow yourself to emerge from this meditation.

6 DIVINE SELF

In the previous chapter, the nature of "Divine Other" is discussed. Spirit is explored in terms of life, consciousness, and male and female aspects. Evolution is discussed as a revelation of Divine purpose in the existence of the universe and life. Transcendence, Grace, and Diversity are also discussed in the context of Divine purpose. The exercise explores whether a person is drawn to an "Earth / Mother / Ruach Breath of Life" manifestation of Divinity or a "Sky / Father / Nephesh Consciousness" manifestation. In the practice, Communion with Divine Other as an unconditionally loving presence is explored.

In this chapter, the nature of human "Self" is explored, in the context of both human and Divine attributes. The concept of "Sacred Core" is developed and discussed in the context of Spiritual maturity. The concept of ego identity is introduced, and the relationship between Sacred Core and ego identities explored. The practice focuses on recognizing "Divine Self Rising."

Narrative:

She had accepted herself as a Divine Child of God, made in the image of God several years ago. The revelation and acceptance helped her through many difficult challenges. It seemed the world was intent on diminishing her sense of self-worth and esteem. Condescending comments from some supervisors, teachers, and family members seemed to pressure her into a "nice girl" template of their making. Having accepted her own inherent Divinity, humanity, and spiritual existence, she cultivated supportive relationships and felt as if she were finally coming in to her own sense of Self, and she liked that feeling.

Then, one day, she witnessed a coworker being criticized for performing a task in the same way that she herself had been congratulated for just the day before. Her coworker had different skin color and ethnicity than herself.

At that moment, she recognized that her self-image as Child of God was only the beginning. To take the next steps, she had to accept herself as an Adult of God, with all the associated privileges and responsibilities. She approached her coworker and supervisor and demonstrated the way she had completed the task the previous day. The supervisor recognized the similarity between her demonstration and her coworker's efforts, and walked away.

Human-Divine Nature

From the perspective of evolution, Divine DNA guides the development of life in the direction of creativity, compassion, love, and community. Similarly, Nephesh consciousness reveals and recognizes movement toward creativity, community, compassion, and unconditional love.

In the Judeo-Christian-Islamic (JCI) account of creation, God Consciousness spoke Creation into existence. When God Ruach breathed life into creation, living creatures emerged. The physical reality of the universe and the carnal life that emerges from within the universe are created in the form and likeness of Divine Being.

In Trinitarian Christian theology, Divinity is described as having three facets or aspects: Divinity, Humanity, and Spirit.

Buddhism also has a trinitarian (trikaya) concept that describes the nature of Buddha in terms of Divinity, Spirituality, and physicality (Padmakara Translation Group, 1997). The aspects or layers of the Buddha-nature are known as "Kaya."

All of this suggests that creation and human evolution follow a "Divine Template." In JCI terms, humanity and creation are made in the image and likeness of God. In Buddhist terms, consciousness is based on an enlightened Buddha-Kaya model.

Of course, being human means having certain limitations, the most obvious being mortality. Like all living things, human beings are mortal and eventually die.

Another limitation of being human comes with having a singular flesh bound existence. Ultimately, every human being is alone. While some people enjoy loving families and close intimate partnerships, everyone, at some point, experiences existential loneliness.

A human being's singular existence also limits the extent to which

71

humans can perceive and understand both the internal universe of consciousness and the external universe of creation and relationships. Human interpretation of self, others, and experience, is limited and subjective.

In contrast, Divinity is usually characterized in terms of immortality or eternal existence (or existence outside of time-space as experienced by the physical universe.) Divinity is also often characterized as having the ability to commune with creation and humanity in a way that transcends the singularity of flesh. Divinity is Ruach Spirit without limit.

Without the limitations associated with singular existence bound in flesh, Divinity has the ability to consciously perceive self and other without subjective interpretation. Divinity is Nephesh Consciousness without limit.

And yet, in communing with the limited existence of creation, life, and humanity, Divinity experiences and understands the limitations of mortality. Divinity participates in the suffering of mortal existence. Divinity has compassion for the human condition.

In this LLCA model, the Sacred Core represents the Divine nature of every human being. Capable of Spiritual communion, the energies that sustain life and consciousness are formed in the image and likeness of Divinity. The Sacred Breeze that passes through Sacred Core cultivates and sustains life and consciousness.

Monistic philosophies characterize Divine Core in terms of Divine Other because in monistic philosophy the differences between Self and Other are illusion. Dualistic philosophies hold that the essence of every human being is unique and separate from all others, Divine or mortal. The nondual understanding of Divine Core recognizes both: participation in Divine Other and unique self-existence.

Like Divinity, humanity can be characterized with a triune nature model. Human beings have life, breath, Ruach. Humans have consciousness, Nephesh, which provides the ability to move, communicate, plan, and create. Humans are also physically carnal with strengths and weaknesses.

Unlike Divinity, human life eventually comes to an end. Human flesh returns to the earth or humus from whence it was formed. While Christian theology believes in Divine Incarnation, the carnal aspect of the human triune nature is limited and subject to suffering. Participation in human existence with limitations and suffering provides a foundation of compassion for and with all other mortal creatures.

Spiritual Maturation

Every human being is sacred, carrying Divine attributes within. In the first chapter, an affirmation is formulated expressing Divine attributes in terms of a parent – child relationship with Higher Power. Every human is a beloved child of God, made in the Image of God.

When a person matures, childhood moves into adulthood. An affirmation that recognizes the power and the responsibility that comes with maturation celebrates adulthood as well. An affirmation that celebrates adulthood also recognizes pronouns associated with adulthood, inclusive to sexual orientation.

"I am a beloved adult person of God, made in the image of God."

"Adult person" can be replaced by whatever pronoun a person uses to describe self. Whatever pronoun a person uses to describe mature self is appropriate to this affirmation. Pronouns like "Cis / Gay / Transgender / Gender Fluid / Exploring / Queer / Lesbian / Bisexual / Nonsexual / Man / Woman" or any combination thereof, or any other word a person uses to describe self can be used in this affirmation.

An affirmation of self does not negate others. To simply say "I am a beloved man of God" or "I am a beloved woman of God" does not negate other sexual orientations, just as saying "I am a beloved Queer of God" of "I am a beloved Lesbian of God" does not negate persons who are cis male and cis female. All people of all orientations are created in the image of God; affirmation of self simply acknowledges and celebrates the aspect of Divinity that each person has an affinity with.

Even as adults, limitations persist that impede the process of maturing into Spiritual adulthood. Confusion, attachments and resentments, aversions and fears, and obsessive and addictive behaviors remain challenges that hold humans back from fulfilling mature, creative, and joy filled potentials.

One might view human behavior from the perspective of carrots and sticks. The most basic carrots are food, water, shelter, safety, and sex. Sticks represent suffering, including suffering resulting from a lack of access to carrots. When people become attached to carrots, they become afraid of sticks. Some people spend entire lifetimes chasing after carrots and avoiding sticks. When obsession with carrots and sticks is released, a certain measure of freedom is experienced. Freedom from attachment includes freedom to fulfill creative potential, to experience and share love, and to share creativity for the benefit of self and others. Freedom from attachment creates opportunity to enjoy Spiritual adulthood.

Children look to parents for fulfilment of needs. Childhood begins with completely dependent relationships with parents and caregivers. In contrast, adult relationships are not dependent; adult relationships are mutually supportive. Physical presence, words and encouragement, and creative gifts are shared with mutual benefit.

Most Spiritual traditions also look to Divine Other for fulfillment of needs. Some describe the relationship between humanity and God as one of complete dependence. A dependent view of faith believes that "faith in Other" provides sustenance needed for both physical and spiritual survival. A dependent view of faith can also be manipulated with fear. An immature faith based on a notion of "complete dependence" can seem threatening and frightening indeed.

Just as healthy parent-child relationships develop into an internalized sense of security and confidence, a spiritual relationship with Higher Power can develop in the same manner. Faith in Other grows and matures to include faith in self.

Faith in self is required for mature adults to take on the responsibilities of caring for self and others, creatively and spiritually. Creative skills are developed, and labors produce fruits which are shared to the mutual benefit of self and others. Human potential is fulfilled.

When the 19th century philosopher Nietzsche suggested that adult humans can reject dependence on the religious dogma of the time, a headline emerged declaring "God is Dead." (Nietzsche, 1883/1995) Thinking and acting as an adult does not kill God. Growing into adulthood fulfills God, even as a child growing into adulthood fulfills the purpose of being a parent.

Spiritual adulthood is not about abandoning faith and becoming completely independent. Spiritual adulthood is about growing into faith that recognizes the limitations of being human and engaging in human relationships. Spiritual adulthood is also about developing faith in self and in communion with Divine Other. Adults become less attached to carrots and sticks, and motivation shifts from fulfilling basic needs to creating and sharing.

Sacred Core and Ego Identities

In the consciousness model, contextual identities are introduced. Identities within human consciousness are said to emerge and "take charge" based on the context a person is engaged in. For example, when caring for children a parenting identity may emerge, and when at work a professional identity may emerge. When danger is perceived, a more primitive identity may emerge from the instinct layer of consciousness, motivating a fight or fight response.

The Sacred Core identity is present also. Similarly, Freud referred to a Super Ego; Buddhism refers to Dharma-Kaya presence, and Christianity refers to a "Divine Seed" that has knowledge of right and wrong. Most people recognize Sacred Core as conscience, but the Sacred Core is much more.

Sacred Core is the Divine manifestation of the triune human. Sacred Core recognizes transcendence beyond the bounds of mortality and physical separation. And, Sacred Core exists in communion with Divine Other, the source of life and consciousness.

Sacred Core may be thought of as the Spiritual "adult in the room" when considered in the context of internal ego identities. When conflicts between identities arise (i.e., "should I attend to my duties as parent or as a professional?"), Sacred Core acts as an arbiter. Sacred Core adds the dimensions of morals and ethics to any decision being made. Sacred Core also provides quiet encouragement and reassurance when circumstances seem out of control. Sacred Core is not a chastising adult, rather Sacred Core is a compassionate and inspiring presence.

Most people experience emotional triggers of some kind or other. Triggers are events or words or even sounds or smells that evoke a strong emotional response. Negative triggers can evoke anger, fear, a sense of helplessness, and other emotions. Positive triggers can evoke joy, passion, and contentment among other emotions. Addiction triggers can evoke a desire to use, drink, or engage in addictive activities such as sex or gambling.

As the "adult in the room," Sacred Core identity has the capacity to be aware of ego and instinct identities that emerge because of triggers. For example, suppose a person experiences a trigger that evokes the emotion of anger. Behind the anger may be an identity of an injured child or a hypervigilant and protective sibling or parent. Given that the response is emotionally strong, the triggered identity likely emerges from the instinct layer. The person experiencing anger is probably not even aware that an identity exists behind this emotion. But the Sacred Core identity, as the adult in the room, is aware. The Sacred Core identity provides a reasoned and compassionate voice saying "Calm down. Consider your options. Impulsive behaviors can cause more harm than good."

Mindfulness helps to amplify the voice of Sacred Core among all other identities. A mindful person in recovery will recognize addiction trigger situations, heed the advice of the Sacred Core identity, and actively defuse or move away from the source of the trigger. Being mindfully aware that the Sacred Core identity is present and provides a calming, reassuring presence can be useful.

Many cultures and religions recognize Sacred Core Identity as being "completely Other." Believing in a calming and reassuring Presence when triggers occur can be very useful. However, believing Sacred Core is completely Other also can foster feelings of dependence and helplessness. For example, a person who believes that an affliction or addiction is purely the result of a struggle between "Divine Will" and "Evil Forces" may also believe that she or he has no agency in life. Lack of agency can create feelings of anxiety and depression, and can discourage a person from actively participating in her or his own recovery and healing.

Other people believe that Sacred Core identity is completely "self," or simply a facet of brain functioning known as consciousness. This can also be calming and reassuring when triggers occur. However, given the very human limitations experienced every day in life, Sacred Core as self alone can also foster a sense of powerlessness. Feeling alone in the midst of suffering can discourage a person from taking active measures toward healing and recovery.

To contrast, Sacred Core Identity recognized as nondual communion of Self and Other can be empowering. As an aspect of Self, Sacred Core has the capacity for active participation in healing. In communion with Divine Other, Sacred Core has access to Divine attributes of patience, love, faith, and hope as resources.

Exercise: Emotional Triggers

For the exercise in this chapter, consider triggers that evoke strong emotions. Keep a journal, recording when strong emotions occur, and note the circumstances that lead to them. Also note the intensity of the emotions on a scale from 1 to 10. Some examples of circumstances that trigger strong emotions include verbal accusations and threats, being ignored, being isolated, loud noises or voices, being in crowded places, and being alone.

If addiction is an issue, list the triggers that evoke the desire to use, drink, or behave in addictive ways. Some examples of addiction triggers include seeing or having access to problem substances, seeing television commercials, associating with other people who have addictive behaviors, or HALT – feeling Hungry, Angry, Lonely, or Tired. If the addictive triggers come from emotional triggers, take another step back and consider the sources of emotional triggers as well.

When recording triggers in a journal, note the time, the location, and any people who are present. Over time, patterns will emerge in the journal. Certain times of day, locations, and perhaps people will be recognized as part of trigger events. Also, record the emotions and the intensity of emotions that occur during the triggers.

Journaling is itself a mindfulness practice that raises awareness of inner processes that evoke outward reactions. Inner processes include inner contextual identities reacting to different situations. The mindfulness gained from journaling awakens Sacred Core Self, which provides both compassion and self-control. Over time, a person may notice that triggers occur less often and with less intensity. With greater mindfulness, Sacred Core Identity is given the opportunity to allow healing to take place.

Practice Preparation: "Rising Up"

Recognizing Sacred Core Self is part of the journey toward developing and sharing creative gifts for the benefit of self and others. As sources of suffering are released, space is made for Sacred Core Self to "rise up" and be a conscious source of motivation, strength, and compassion.

The "rising up" metaphor has been used to describe the development of human potential in both psychological models and in spiritual traditions. In the 1940's Dr. Abraham Maslow represented human development as a triangular "hierarchy of needs", building from a solid foundation at the bottom. (Maslow, 1943)

Figure 7: Hierarchy of Needs

In Maslow's model several layers are described, which can be broken down into three basic areas. The base of the triangle illustrates that survival needs must be met before further development is possible. While creativity plays a role in meeting survival needs, a person cannot reach her or his creative potential without having access to clean water, healthy nutrition, and comfortable shelter.

After basic survival needs are met, a person has an expanded capacity to connect with and care for others. Healthy relationships help to build self-confidence as well. While creativity plays a role in connecting with others and building healthy relationships, reaching one's creative potential requires the help and support of others.

Having met survival needs, formed healthy relationships, and developed a sense of autonomy and confidence, a person can develop and share creative gifts to the benefit of self and others. For Maslow, the joy of creative engagement that is productive and shared is the epitome of human existence.

Many Spiritual traditions also recognize the "rising up" metaphor for human development. Life and humanity rise up from the earth in Native American, African, Japanese, and other spiritual traditions. In the JCI spiritual tradition, Divine Ruach is breathed into inert humus or earth, from which life and humanity arise and develop. One might easily infer that the shared "rising up" metaphor for life and humanity suggests a common Nephesh Consciousness inspiration.

During the practice for this chapter, Divine Self is recognized. While previous practices have worked in a "top down" fashion, moving from mind, to heart, to core, to root, this practice begins at the root chakra. This practice visualizes Divine Self -Rising.

During the self-emptying practice, the challenges of confusion, attachments and resentments, fears, and unhealthy obsessions are released. After that, Divine Other is invited to fill the vacated spaces with hope and clarity, love, faith, and joy. During this Divine Self-Rising practice, Divine attributes are claimed as part of self. Created in the image of the Divine, Divine characteristics are part of human nature.

Sacred Core represents Divine Potential for every human being. In a way, Sacred Core represents "True Self," the realization of Divine Potential. Recognizing and embracing Divine Potential can be very uplifting.

Practice:

As always, this practice starts with establishing a solid and comfortable posture, breathing from the diaphragm, and focusing on breath. Having experienced the previous practices many times, you can pass through them quickly. Starting at the outermost layer of waking consciousness, breathe and release your thoughts. Next, breathe again, recognize, and release subconscious identities and feelings. With one more breath, recognize and release the instincts that represent the carrots and sticks to which you normally respond.

Stepping into your Sacred Core, take a moment to breath. Recognize the sacred breezes that flow, supporting life and consciousness.

Focusing on your mind, breathe and surrender any confusing distractions. Moving attention to your heart, breathe and surrender any attachments or resentments. Moving attention to your core, release aversions and fears. Finally move attention into your root, breathe, and surrender any obsessions or guilt.

Recognize and enjoying this moment of complete emptiness, complete freedom. Embrace pure awareness. If needed, you can take a moment to recognize and release sources of physical and emotional pain as well.

Now move attention back to your mind chakra and with a cleansing breath, invite Divine Clarity to provide guidance. Moving attention into your heart, breathe and invite Divine Love to provide fulfillment. Moving attention to your core, breathe and invite Divine Faith to provide inspiration. Finally, move attention into your root chakra, breathe, and invite Divine joy, motivation, and creativity to flourish.

Rested now and relaxed, recognize the earth to which you are connected. Solid, grounded, and real, this is the foundation from which life emerges and flourishes. This is the place from which life arose at the beginning. This is your connection with humus, earth, and humanity. This realization can be humbling. You are an integral part of all physical reality, life, and humanity.

Moving attention to your root chakra, imagine a glowing warmth developing. The root is the Divine source of life and creativity. Like a newborn drawing first breath, Divine Self emerges within your root with great passion, motivation for existence, and the will to thrive. With every inhale, the warmth and glow within your root increases, along with your sense of creative joy and passion. Motivation to develop and share creative potential emerges. With every breath, recognize the warm glow of motivation increasing within your root. With every breath, the sensation of warmth grows stronger. The warmth and glow emanating from your root eventually touches your core chakra.

Imagine a glowing warmth now kindled within your core. Your core chakra adds the energy of faith to the motivation and passion already experienced. The wisdom you have gathered from experience is recognized. From the moment of your birth, both positive and negative experiences have contributed to your wisdom. With every breath, the warmth and glow of self-confidence grows. Rest for a moment in your core, breathing, and accepting a growing realization of faith. Eventually, the warmth and glow within your core touches your heart chakra.

Breathe and imagine a warm glow being kindled within your heart. Along with motivation and faith, there is love. Love for self, love for others, love for Divine Other all reside within the warm glow. With every breath, the warmth and the glowing light grow stronger. Compassion, kindness, and patience are recognized, which are further signs of spiritual maturation. With Divine Other present in loving communion, recognize the presence of love that does not control, but inspires. Love and compassion give life meaning and purpose that transcends mere existence. The presence of motivation from the root and self-confidence from the core are now fulfilled with meaning and purpose that only love can provide. Intentional resting and breathing allow the warmth and glow of the heart to touch your mind chakra.

Now within your mind chakra, every breath increases the warmth and glow. Divine awareness is kindled, along with clarity of vision. Life and existence can be experienced without filters and limits. Motivation, confidence, and purpose energy from the lower chakras inform the mind, enhancing self-awareness. Creative gifts and abilities, and the will to develop and share them become apparent. Growth into spiritual adulthood is completed. Allow yourself to breathe and dwell within the mind chakra for several minutes.

Life, Breath, Ruach energy flows from Mother Earth, sustaining and nurturing life. Nephesh Consciousness energy flows from Father Sky, bringing awareness and vision. Divine life and consciousness energies flow in nondual communion with Divine Self. The warmth and glow that emanates from all internal chakras spreads to fill your entire body. Visualize yourself glowing with creativity, motivation, and purpose, and radiating hope, faith, and love. As the warmth and glow of awareness intensifies throughout your body, recognize the vast expanse of possibilities for development and growth. Opportunities seem endless. With Divine Other flowing in nondual communion with Divine Self, recognize joyful motivation, faith inspired confidence, love centered purpose, and hope centered vision. Recognize that anything is possible.

Now slowly, slowly return attention to your breathing. Feelings of peace and gratitude abound.

Extending your gratitude outward, imagine health and well-being for self and those near at hand, including neighbors and townspeople. Extend positive intentions outward, throughout your county or parish, your state or province, and your national affiliation. Finally, extend positive intentions to the entire world. Peace and love for all people, all living creatures, the environment, and all of creation.

7 COMPASSION FOR SELF

In the previous chapter, human development is explored from the perspective of the "Image of God." Existential limitations associated with being human are discussed, as is the nature of "Sacred Core." Spiritual maturity is described, as well as the relationship between Sacred Core and Identity Egos. In the practice, Divine Self is developed with energy centers providing motivation, self-confidence, love centered purpose, and clarity of vision.

In this chapter, existential limitations associated with being human are further explored. Acceptance and compassion are described as ways of dealing with existential realities. Concepts of debt, guilt, compassion, and forgiveness, are explored. Given the challenges and suffering associated with human existence, the practice focuses on compassion for self.

Narrative

He was well past middle aged. When he thought back on his life, he recognized some successes, some failures, and some occasions where he had fallen short. He carried guilt for the occasions where his skills and resources were inadequate to meet the needs of others and himself. Compromises had been made. Others had been hurt along the way. He had missed opportunities to share love and be fully present.

As a child, his life had been less than ideal. While there had been love, there were also painful experiences, losses, and neglect. He recognized that his parents had been dealing with challenges of their own. He had truly and sincerely forgiven them for the suffering he experienced as a child, and carried gratitude for the foundation and legacy of longsuffering love they had provided.

Sighing, he realized there was nothing he could do to change the past. He recognized that the only path forward was to accept the past, to have compassion for the challenges and suffering common to every human being, and to celebrate love. He chose forgiveness, for himself and all others. Childhood vulnerability, and the indiscretion, impulsivity, and ignorance of youth and young adulthood, as well as the joyful and painful experiences he had shared, were all part of the journey and the adventure. The wisdom and compassion he carried represented the culmination of his experiences.

Human Existential Limitations

Realizing Divine Self can be a very uplifting experience, which is the reason that many practices and programs are geared toward realizing some form of Divine Self, Enlightenment, or Self Actualization. After participating in Divine Self oriented programs, participants tend to feel uplifted and positive.

However, no matter how uplifting the experience or training, reality has a way of weaving itself back into a person's life. Yes, humans are in part Divine, and yet, humanity remains human. The existential realities of mortality and loneliness remain in some form, even for the most enlightened individuals.

People who participate in programs and practices exclusively pursuing some form of Spiritual Enlightenment while ignoring existential realities engage in what is called Spiritual Bypassing. Spiritual Bypassing is a term sometimes used to describe ignoring reality and suffering in the world, while pursuing some sort of spiritual purity. Ignoring suffering of self and others does not make the suffering go away.

When this realization hits, people react in various ways. Some persist in denying the realities associated with being human. Some get angry, while others get depressed. Some abandon and renounce their practices and often try something else. Throughout their lifetimes, many people try a variety of activities with the hope of mitigating existential suffering. Examples include social worship, joining a gym, exploring dietary supplements, taking up yoga, and trying a variety of other forms of spiritual engagement. Pursuing a variety of activities and practices can be very educational and helpful, but no matter the practice, existential realities stubbornly persist.

Perhaps there is no "cure" for being human, but there is a balm that can help soothe the pain of loss and loneliness. The balm is compassion.

Compassion for self involves accepting the limitations of being human. Humanity is constrained by existential limitations of mortality and being physically separated from the universe and everyone in it. Humanity is also subject to errors in judgment and actions that result in harm to self and others.

Most spiritual traditions and religions provide definitions or guidelines for what it means to be a "good" person. These guidelines tie directly into the idealized identities that guide day to day thoughts and actions. For example, the Jain culture holds a "good" standard of harming no living creatures. For a Jain, simply swatting a mosquito creates a disconnect with the idealized standard, which results in emotional discomfort. (Long, 2013)

In most traditions and cultures, the compliance or violation of culturally established rules of good and bad behavior are thought to directly affect a person's existential status. In some traditions, the existential limitations of being human are amplified in an attempt to control good vs bad behaviors. For example, in some cultures if a person is "bad" the existential inevitability of death is exacerbated to include an eternity of suffering, either in tormenting flames or in an endless cycle of suffering reincarnations. On the other hand, a "good" person has the opportunity not only to avoid mortality and live forever, but to also avoid existential separation and live in a state of eternal communion with loving Divinity.

Despite the existential carrots and sticks offered in cultures and religions, the human condition persists here and now. Humans experience mortality in loss and separation every day. Worldwide, about 0.8% of the population dies every year, which translates to over 150 thousand human deaths every day (World Bank Group, 2022). There is much suffering, separation, and grief, even without the burden of culturally imposed threats and rewards beyond mortality.

Because suffering persists here and now and because many cultural promises and prescriptions for suffering tend to focus on "after-life" rather than on here and now, compassion is worth consideration as a balm for easing the here and now effects of existential suffering.

Compassion and Forgiveness

What is compassion? When broken down, the word compassion literally means "suffering with." Compassion is simply the act of being fully present and connecting with another person's suffering. Anyone who has given or received compassion knows this to be true. Whether taking the time to sit with someone who is ill or is grieving, or simply sending cards or flowers, letting a person know that he or she is not alone and that someone cares can help ease suffering.

While compassion is an act of being present, forgiving is an act of pardoning an offense. If, for example, a person loans another person money, the receiving person receives money, and the lending person carries a note of promise for the eventual return of the money. The relationship of debt is a burden for both the person receiving the loan and the lender who holds the note.

While debts and notes associated with money are straightforward, debts and notes associated with intangible losses are more difficult to manage. For example, if one person injures another, the injured person carries an intangible note of promise for compensation against the person who causes the injury. Jewish scripture and laws attempt to establish a rate of exchange for resolving intangible debt, but the intangible nature of suffering and loss makes any physical compensation inadequate. "Eye for an Eye" does not bring healing. (Tanakh, 1985 Lev. 24:19-21) An emotion often associated with carrying a note of intangible compensation is "resentment."

If a person who causes an injury has any capacity for compassion, the burden of the intangible debt is carried by him or her as well. The emotion often associated with carrying intangible debt is "guilt."

An injured person can find relief from resentment by forgiving the person who inflicted the injury. Forgiving another person, or letting go of the intangible note, is not necessarily easy. Like grieving, forgiving involves a process that takes time and acceptance. Forgiving does not imply that an injury never happened, nor that an injury may never happen again. Forgiving is simply the process of releasing the note related to an injury or loss.

Even if an injured person truly forgives another, the burden of guilt on the part of the injuring party may persist. Whether an act of inflicting injury is accidental or intentional, guilt associated with intangible debt may persist. To resolve an intangible debt, a person must forgive herself / himself. Like laying down a note, the process of forgiving self, or letting go of an intangible debt, requires time and acceptance. Forgiving self does not forget the injury, nor does it allow for further injury to occur.

For both a person holding on to the intangible guilt of having inflicted loss or injury, and for a person holding resentment associated with loss or injury, burdens can only be mitigated through compassion and forgiveness.

Note the difference between compassion and forgiveness: compassion is the capacity to empathize with suffering, while forgiveness is the act of letting go of intangible debt. Compassion is a prerequisite for forgiveness. Compassion is a prerequisite for healing.

Without compassion, the holders of notes and debts, with each their own associated resentments and guilt, would never be relieved of those burdens. Both the note holder and the debt holder need compassion for both self and other for complete forgiveness, reconciliation, and healing to take place.

Notice that an actual exchange of note for debt is not really possible. An injury cannot be taken back, and an intangible note cannot be given in return. Even if a verbal exchange of forgiveness takes place, or some kind of monetary or property exchange is performed as an act of compensation there is no guarantee that both parties will lay down their respective emotional burdens at the time of exchange.

For a successful exchange that releases intangible debt, both parties must be willing and able to release all resentment and guilt. If one party is not willing, the other would be forced to carry the burden of resentment and guilt toward self or other for the rest of his or her life. While the mutual release of burden is ideal, the release of guilt and resentment requires time. Healing of relationship requires time. And people move through the process of releasing guilt and resentment at different rates, if they can do so at all. Mutual release of intangible burdens in any sort of exchange at any specific time and place is difficult at best.

Everyone suffers emotional slights and injuries. Everyone suffers physical injuries. At some point in life everyone inflicts injuries on self and others, whether intentionally or unintentionally. Everyone experiences guilt and resentment as a result of inflicting or receiving injury. Because everyone experiences suffering, guilt, and resentment, everyone has the capacity for compassion when encountering suffering, guilt, and resentment. And where there is capacity for compassion, there is capacity for forgiving.

Existential Suffering

Specific injury, whether emotional or physical, unintentional or intentional, can be forgiven. Resentment and guilt can be released with willingness, acceptance, and time. But the existential challenges of being human, including suffering, separation, loss, and loneliness, can be more challenging. Who does one forgive?

Most, if not all religious traditions place the blame for being human squarely on the shoulders of humanity. Various traditions suggest blaming and punishing people for being weak and inadequate; for being mortal and fallible. Some ovations are made to assign blame to malicious supernatural entities. Similar ovations appeal to supernatural entities for advocacy and redemption. While appeals to Divine Other can bring comfort and inspire a person to pursue and accept compassion and forgiveness, the process of sharing compassion and forgiveness is still necessary for some measure of healing and reconciliation. Using spirituality to bypass human emotions and to avoid compassion and forgiveness can result in lingering resentments and guilt.

In previous chapters, the hypothesis was proposed that humanity is evolving toward greater compassion, community, and love both organically and sociologically. The idea of Divine Spirit having the properties of Ruach or breath / life, and Nephesh Consciousness, was discussed in the context of Divine Spirit.

Theistic traditions believe that Higher Power created the universe and all that is in it. But if a powerful, benevolent, and loving Higher Power created the universe, how can mortal suffering exist, especially when those who suffer are often blameless? This is perhaps the oldest and most vexing question that has faced theologians and philosophers since the beginning of time. The problem of a "good" Creator allowing "bad" to happen in creation is called "theodicy."

Existential suffering associated with separation and mortality can also be interpreted in terms of debts and notes. As is the case with specific instances of injury, existential debts and notes are intangible. Whether an injury exists between humans, between Deity and humanity, or between a natural processes like earthquakes and humanity, any injury or loss related debts and notes are intangible. The assignment of blame, guilt, and associated resentment is intangible. Existential suffering from death and separation is very real, but any associated blame or possible recompense is intangible.

As is the case with debts and notes between individuals, the balm for existential suffering is compassion, and the cure is forgiveness for self and Other, even if the Other is Divine.

At some point in life, everyone loses someone important to them, which usually brings resentment against some form of Divine Other. Unfortunately, most cultures and religions consider holding such resentments taboo. As a result, suffering of loss and injury can be compounded not only with resentment, but also with guilt.

Mustering a sense of compassion for an all-powerful Deity who allows injury and suffering can be difficult. If one assumes that Divine Other is benevolent, then one must acknowledge that for every existential loss or injury, Divine Other carries a note for each loss or injury. The idea of a Divine Benevolent Other carrying notes against suffering that has occurred in the entire universe since the beginning of time can be humbling. To carry such a burden would require nothing less that Divine Compassion and a Divine ability to forgive Self and others.

Believing that Benevolent Divine Other holds compassion for all suffering can be powerful. Believing that God suffers with creation as injuries and losses occur can evoke a sense of profound gratitude and even compassion for God. Recognizing that Higher Power may be a compassionate presence during suffering can be comforting. People with faith often testify to the sense of comforting Presence during difficult times.

While compassion directed toward Other can be difficult, compassion directed toward self can be even more difficult. Childhood, culture, tradition, and religion are all riddled with accusations of human unworthiness. Selfless service is often demanded, but self-care is often neglected in cultural norms and sacred scriptures. Expectations are embedded in societal ideals for how a "good woman" and a "good man" must provide service in relationships and in society, without regard to meeting self-care and self-esteem needs.

For this reason, cultivating a sense of sacred self-worth can be incredibly powerful. With the practice of "Divine Self-Rising," the identity of Sacred Core Self is established. And Sacred Core Self has the capacity for compassion for the debts and notes accumulated as part of being human.

Compassion for self has more benefit than easing the burden of existential loss and suffering. Compassion for self provides a foundation for cultivating compassion for others. Compassion for others will be explored in later sections as the consciousness plane is expanded to include relationships.

Exercise: Debts and Notes

As an exercise, consider the ways you may have been hurt or injured by others. Also consider the ways you may have caused injury to self or others. When considering intangible debts and notes, people often put a great deal of energy into justification. For example, a person might think "Well, yes, I caused suffering in this instance, but it was due to these circumstances." Try to avoid putting energy into rationalizing and justifying. As with other exercises, just brainstorm. When incidents of emotional or physical hurt pop up in your mind, just write them down. This is an awareness building exercise in preparation for the practice.

Try not to dwell on the Other, whether human, Divine, or even circumstance that either caused or received physical or emotion injury. For now, the exercise is focused on the feelings of resentment and guilt that accumulate within self.

If this exercise proves difficult, consider doing the exercise with someone who is supportive. As with any exercise, if the practice proves too difficult or painful, just set it down and move on. The program is designed to help, not hurt.

Received Injury, Note, or Resentment	Inflicted Injury, Debt, or Guilt

While doing the exercise, you may notice that one column has many more entries than the other. This is useful information for building mindfulness. Some people tend to accumulate guilt while not recognizing or acknowledging their own suffering. Other people tend to carry resentments without considering the suffering they may have caused others. Notice whether a tendency to justify or rationalize any imbalance occurs. Try not to judge; this exercise is simply information to be considered without judgment toward self or others.

Practice Preparation:

In previous sessions, a process of recognizing and releasing emotions was discussed. In this session, rather than releasing emotions, emotions are simply accepted. Compassion is a process of presence and acceptance without judgment.

When existential challenges like illness, loneliness, or loss occur, faith in Divine Other can be comforting and helpful. Many people turn to the "power of prayer" for aid in dealing with existential issues.

While prayers can be comforting and helpful, actual resolution of suffering can be elusive. Most circumstances cannot be "controlled through prayer." For example, most people in recovery will testify that addiction cannot be "controlled through prayer."

Mature faith recognizes that while control is not possible, believing in Compassionate Presence of Divine Other can provide comfort and resilience. In recovery, "Higher Power" is an inspiring presence. Many addicts reach a point where they have alienated almost every human being in their lives. When existential realities of loneliness and mortality are most evident and prevalent, compassionate Divine Presence is recognized.

In recovery groups, people recognize the power of presence. Whether in AA, NA, meditation, or faith-based recovery groups, the underlying principles are the same. While encouraging presence and occasional friendly advice are appreciated, self-control is up to the individual. After finally accepting the reality and challenges of addiction, and after finally choosing to accept help, many people recognize Higher Power working through the compassionate presence and encouragement of others.

The illustration of addiction and recovery is used to demonstrate the empowering nature of presence over control. The benefits of acceptance and recognition of compassionate presence outside of self are not limited to addiction and recovery, people who suffer chronic pain, disability, and mental health issues can benefit as well. Simply being human is a chronic condition that involves suffering, loss, and loneliness. Acceptance of compassionate presence is where healing begins. Control may provide short term fixes, but presence inspires self-care.

Understanding that Divine Other chooses compassionate presence over control can provide a sense of companionship and empowerment for moving forward in life, even when physical, emotional, and / or spiritual challenges are present. Similarly, supportive friends provide encouragement and compassionate presence rather than control. Although a good friend at the right place and time might help "clear the way" for healing to take place, taking the steps of seeking out and accepting help is ultimately up to the individual.

Divine Presence is not obvious, especially when a person is suffering. Divine Presence may be discerned through open eyes, ears, and hearts. The self-emptying practice described in Chapter 3 can be very helpful in clearing out the attachments, fears, and distractions that can make Divine Presence hard to discern.

Divine Self flows within the Divine Core, and exists in living breathing communion with Divine Other. Understanding that Divine Self abides in nondual communion with Divine Other is part of this and other compassion-oriented practices. Communion of Self and Other is a partnership that transcends the human condition and limitations.

This self-compassion practice is similar to the self-emptying practice, as it descends through the chakras. However, rather than focusing on surrendering challenges, in this practice challenges are viewed through Divine Eyes with compassion. Divine Presence recognizes human challenges without judgment, rationalization, or efforts to change or control. Divine Self is simply present with Human self.

Some might interpret this part of the practice as a private "pity party," which is not only unproductive, but also can lead to a sense of helplessness. The difference between a pity party and compassion for self is that one's humanity is recognized through newly discovered Divine Eyes. Taking the "Divine perspective" allows a person to observe from a more objective point of view. Divine perspective allows a person to accept and to be fully present.

As with any practice, self-care and safety are important. The real work of practice often happens between practice sessions. Challenging feelings and memories may arise. Supportive friends, family, Spiritual Discernment, and therapeutic resources are important to have available as challenges and emotions are processed between meditation sessions.

Practice

Begin with a comfortable and upright meditative posture, breathing with your diaphragm. Deep breathing relaxes and allows release of distractions. Imagine that stray thoughts and feelings dissipate with every exhale, while every inhale brings soothing relief. Your breath is your safe space; it is always present.

Imagine the space your root chakra occupies. Imagine Divine energy, Ruach life energy, rising up from the earth to bring warmth and energy to your root chakra. As the warmth and positive energy grows, feel yourself respond with a sense of joy and enthusiasm. Recognize that this energy represents the breath of life rising from the earth, animating, and rejuvenating. Recognize the feeling of motivation that accompanies this energy.

Move your attention up to your core chakra. Feel the energy in the root chakra rising upward, warming your core. Feel yourself respond with a sense of faith and strength. Recognize faith in yourself, faith in your Higher Power, and recognize your creative gifts available for your benefit and the benefit of others. The feeling of self-confidence accompanies root chakra energy.

Moving upward to the heart chakra, recognize Divine Love blossoming like a flower. Recognize your Divine purpose in this, to love and to share love with others. Feel your heart begin to glow with Divine Love.

Now move your attention to your mind. Feel your mind opening to a light from above, Divine Nephesh Consciousness. Visualize clouds dissipating as your mind gains clarity. Recognize creativity being released, given free rein to learn, explore, and grow,

Recognize Divine Nephesh Energy descending into your heart chakra. In the heart, Nephesh Consciousness meets Ruach Life in loving embrace. Recognize the heart as the place where Nephesh Consciousness, Ruach Life-Breath, and material existence meet in a trinity of lifegiving love.

Feel the Divine Breeze flow through your core, from Sky to earth and earth to sky, Ruach and Nephesh energies flowing in communion with Divine self. Recognize the clarity, the love, the strength, and the creative joy that is part of you.

Take a moment to just sit and breathe, allowing yourself to feel the flow of energy. Joy, hope, faith, and love flood your senses. With Divine Self in communion with Divine Other, you are fully present.

Now, with a sense of humility and compassion, begin the process of recognizing your human self. Imagine your Divine Eyes looking upon your human self with a sense of love and compassion.

Imagine the area your mind occupies, and recall the conflicting messages your mind processes every day. Recall the sense of confusion you sometimes feel. Allow Divine Self to be an understanding presence, recognizing the very human challenges you face every day. Without judgment, without attempts to fix or release any thoughts, just accept yourself with compassion. Breathe and be fully present. Like a healing balm, let every breath simply acknowledge your human challenges without condition and without judgment.

Allow your Divine self to be fully present with your human mind. Every breath is filled with compassion and understanding. Recognize the impatience of youth and the diminishing capacity that sometimes happens with age. The human mind has limits, and the Divine Self understands. Every breath brings comfort in recognizing the Divine capacity for compassion, for presence, and for acceptance.

Allow your attention to move to your heart. Recognize the human dimensions of your heart. Recognize the scars and resentments that are still present. Every breath brings understanding and acceptance. Simply be fully present with yourself. Your human self has experienced losses, and your divine self understands. Your human self has both given and received injuries and hurts. Divine self does not judge nor try to fix anything; Divine self is simply present. All feelings and attachments are part of the human condition. Divine Self knows and accepts this, and responds with compassion.

Divine self is fully present with your human heart. Complex feelings of grief, guilt, love, and need are all met with compassion. Divine Self has the capacity to love without condition. From the struggles of childhood, to the relationships of youth, and onward through maturation, Divine Self understands the experience of human emotions. Divine Self also understands feelings of loneliness. Divine Self responds with unconditional love. Take time to breathe; take time to give and receive love.

Now allow your attention to move downward to your core. Divine presence recognizes the human capacity for fear. Divine Wisdom understands and accepts this very human emotion. Let every breath provide a comforting balm to soothe your human fears. Recognize that strength grows from acceptance.

Divine self understands the human desire to avoid the hurts that come with human existence. Divine self does not judge. Some of the habits and behaviors that have accumulated through life are part of this avoidance. Divine self understands. Divine self has compassion for the human condition and all the hurts, loneliness, and losses that are part of the human condition. From the hurts of youth to the loneliness and losses that come with maturation, Divine Self understands and accepts complex feelings that arise in the core. Divine self loves your humanity. Allow yourself to breathe in acceptance, breathe in compassion, and simply sit with yourself in compassion.

Now move your attention to the root chakra. Divine presence understands human passions. Divine self recognizes human impulsivity. Divine presence understands human obsessions. Divine presence does not judge. Divine Self is simply present. Compassionate. And still. Recognize every breath as a healing balm.

Passion and desire for control are part of the human condition. Let every breath bring acceptance and comfort. Being human can be challenging and difficult; Divine presence understands. Allow yourself to breathe for several minutes, simply accepting yourself, and loving yourself.

Now move your attention to your entire being, to your entire self. Look at yourself through your Divine eyes, with acceptance and Grace. You are human, and you are loved. All the physical, emotional, and spiritual challenges you experience are part of your human existence. You are accepted and loved, without judgment or condition. Divine self is simply present and understanding. Breathe through this; accept this. This is powerful knowledge. Human existence is hard. Divine Presence understands. Mistakes are made. Divine presence understands.

You may dwell in this place of peaceful acceptance and compassion for some time, just breathing, recognizing, and accepting with love. Then, with gratitude, return attention to your breathing. You are fully present. You are grounded. You are fully human. You are Divine. And you are loved.

A true sense of humility and gratitude rises up. Positive intentions toward self and positive intentions toward others emerges. Recognize the common humanity of family, friends, and neighbors. Positive intentions toward others are filled with compassion. All living creatures and even plants experience the joys and the challenges associated with living. Widening your attention, allow positive intentions to expand toward others in your local town, your state or province, and again expand to include positive intentions toward your nation of residence. Finally, allow your positive intentions and compassion to extend outward to include everyone in the world.

Breathing, relaxed, emerge from your meditation. Take a step back and look at your fully human self as a whole being. Yes, confusion, attachments, aversions, and obsessions are still present. And yes, there is clarity; there is love; there is faith; and there is joy. Recognize how your human self exists in nondual communion with Divine Self and Divine Other.

8 EXPANDING CONSCIOUSNESS

As a framework for developing self-awareness, this program introduces models for consciousness, identity, and chakra energy flows. In the previous chapter, the concepts of debt, forgiveness, and guilt are explored in the context of intangible suffering and loss. The concepts of debt and forgiveness are expanded to include the existential challenges that are common to humanity and all living creatures. In the instruction and in the practice, compassion for self is cultivated as a foundation for forgiving self and cultivating compassion and forgiveness for others.

In this chapter, the consciousness plane and Sacred Core energy centers are reviewed with a goal of expanding Sacred Core energy into consciousness layers. Addiction is described as an obsessive focus that impedes and neglects holistic chakra energy flow. The relationship between obsessive energy focus and addictive ego identity is discussed, and human limitations are described in terms of motivation for creative energy development.

Narrative:

It was one of those days. Her sales numbers were down month on month, her husband and children were demanding attention, and she had missed her yoga class for the third time in a row. Since the financial markets had begun to fall, sales were off for everyone, but that brought little solace. While her bosses and coworkers were understanding, she could read the concern in their faces, for everyone. They all had families, they all needed their jobs to support their families, and her family was no exception. What she really wanted to do was to find a cozy bar, a glass of wine,

96

and a cigarette. Recognizing her rising urges, she closed her eyes for a moment and focused on her breathing. She recognized the voices inside her demanding attention. The good employee voice was dominant at the moment, but the good mother and good wife voices clamored for attention as well. She also recognized the voices of fear that called her to run away and retreat into comforting old habits. Continuing to breathe, she found the deeper, still, small voice within her, filled with compassion. With that voice came a wave of patience and wisdom, calling her to accept her circumstances with compassion, and simply be present. She knew that the voices of fear were really calling out for self-care. She also knew she had friends she could count on to be present when her peace was threatened.

Looking at her calendar, she intentionally cleared time for meeting her own needs, with friends and yoga and just walking in the park. She created intentional times and spaces to be present for her family and her most demanding clients as well. She recognized that she could do this, one day at a time, one hour at a time, and one minute at a time.

Holistic Energy Consciousness Model

The human consciousness model presented in Chapter 2 includes waking consciousness, a subconscious that contains an internal representation of the universe and multiple situational identities, a neurochemical instinct layer, and a Sacred Core.

Physical Boundary
Waking Consciousness
Subconsciousness
Neurochemical - Instinct
Sacred Core

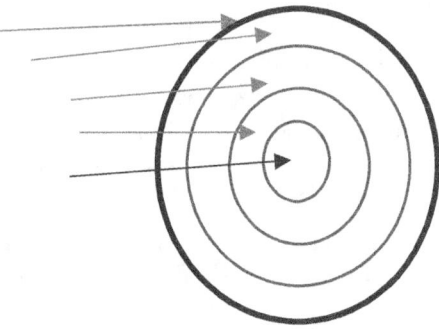

Figure 8: Human Consciousness Model

The Sacred Core energy centers introduce in chapter 3 include: the mind chakra associated with clarity and creativity, the heart chakra associated with love, the core chakra associated with faith and self-confidence, and the root chakra associated with passion and joy.

A correlation is also introduced between Sacred Core chakra energy centers and neurochemicals produced within the instinct layer of consciousness. The mind chakra is associated with creativity-oriented endocannabinoids and clarity-oriented dopamine. The heart chakra is associated with relationship supporting oxytocin. The core chakra, located in the region of the diaphragm, connects with confidence and calm producing serotonin, and the root chakra located toward the base of the spine with passion and joy producing endorphins. The mnemonic introduced for these neurochemicals is EDOSE.

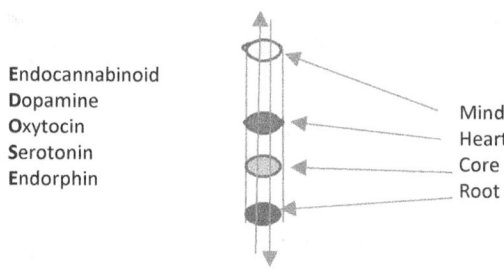

Figure 9: Neurochemical Energy Layers

The correlation between Sacred Core spiritual energy centers and instinct layer neurochemicals extends to the subconscious and waking consciousness layers as well. Clarity, love, faith and wisdom, and joyful enthusiasm flow through core, instinct, subconscious, and waking conscious layers. With sacred energy flowing throughout the layers of consciousness, all layers and all levels work together to create a fulfilled human experience. With the inclusion of Spiritual energy centers, the consciousness model represents a holistic system.

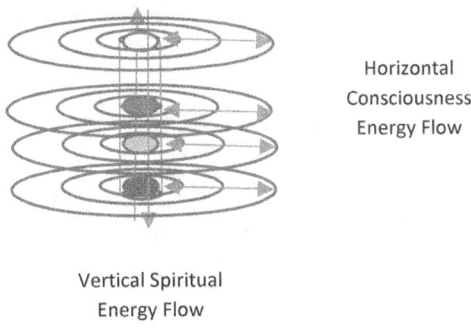

Horizontal
Consciousness
Energy Flow

Vertical Spiritual
Energy Flow

Figure 10: Holistic Consciousness Model

Situational and Sacred Core Identities

The concept of identity archetypes or standards is introduced in Chapter 2. Different identity standards exist for different contexts. Examples of identity standards include good parent, good worker, and good student.

When identity standards become internalized, they help form distinct aspects of who a person is. One way to model human consciousness is as a collection of identities that respond to different situations or circumstances. (Schwartz, 2001). Examples of situations where specific identities respond include parenting, working at professions, various activities, and in relationships.

With multiple identities available for different situations, it is inevitable that conflicts arise when multiple situations develop simultaneously. For example, a parent identity may find herself negotiating with an occupational identity if a child needs assistance at school during a work day.

While situational identities emerge from the subconscious layer, protector identities emerge from within the instinct layer. Using the prior example, while parent and identity models negotiate for dominance, a protector identity considers whether the child is injured or in danger and whether that danger may extend to self. If a protector identity determines that danger is present, the protector identity will take control of the situation and both parent and worker identities will take a back seat. Using the example, of the child is injured or in danger at school, the parent may leave her job without telling anyone and rush to the side of her child.

With all these identities operating in parallel, one might ask the question, who is the real person? Outside of all these internal identities the world sees a single person, but who is this person? The world identifies this person with a name, like John, Eric, Jane, or Beatrice for example. And yet, really knowing John, Jane, Eric, or Beatrice means knowing that each is a person with far more attributes and gifts than meet the eye. Each person has families, friends, interests, and occupations. Each person is multi-faceted. Each person is human. Each person makes mistakes and suffers illness, aging, loneliness, and all the challenges associated with being human. Each person is also sacred, creative, and divine.

The Sacred Core serves as the central locus identity for every human being. All other facets, aspects, and identities exist in relation to the Sacred Core. While interaction with another person may involve an interplay of different context dependent identities, the central person is projected from that person's Sacred Core.

Obsession Related Energy Flow

Chapter 2 describes the Sacred Core having Chakras or energy centers that source characteristics like vision, love, confidence, and enthusiasm. When all energy centers flow freely in communion with Divine Other, the effects of the Divine flow can be seen throughout the layers of consciousness. The effects can be seen in a person's life and livelihood and relationships. Motivation, self-confidence, love, and creative vision are all part of a holistic, joyful life.

While freely flowing energy centers from within the Sacred Core are possible, energy flows can sometimes be limited. When a person becomes focused on or obsessed with any one particular energy center and its associated neurochemical, imbalance occurs. When this happens, flow from other chakra energy centers become constricted.

Obsessions can manifest as addiction to a substance or behavior. Obsessions can also manifest as relationship or control issues.

For example, the mind centered energy is associated with dopamine. Addiction to a stimulant like cocaine causes a large amount of dopamine to flood the nervous system. Concurrently, mind centered chakra energy dominates the Sacred Core. As a result, heart, core, and root chakra energies are restricted. A person who is addicted to cocaine eventually loses interest in other energy center related activities like relationships, sleep, and even sex. All creativity is dedicated to obtaining the substance of choice.

Obsessions with gambling, shopping, hoarding, and other behaviors also create surges of dopamine which over time have similar detrimental effects on holistic energy flow.

Marijuana, a hallucinogen, can also be associated with the mind chakra and with the endocannabinoid neurochemical. Over use of weed (or gummies) can eventually sap motivation and relationships, rendering faith and creative energies impotent. (*Author's note: One of the lessons learned in working with addiction is "never argue with weed people." There are numerous studies promoting the benefits of marijuana, and there are certainly flawed studies demonizing its use. The bottom line remains that externally introduced substances mimic neurochemicals that the body produces naturally. In working with addiction clients, I have observed the effects of clouded reason, reduced motivation, and enhanced paranoia, especially in heavy smokers and users.)

Opioids bind with endorphin neuroreceptors and disrupt the natural flow of endorphins for managing pain and experiencing passion and joy. Root chakra energy dominates, restricting creative vision, relationships, and the ability to feel at peace. Obsession with sex and pornography also creates addictive surges in endorphins, which also disrupt creativity, relationships, and peace of mind.

Alcohol and other depressants provide a chemically induced sense of both euphoria and relaxation. In alcohol addiction, dominant core chakra energy eventually disrupts creativity and vision, relationships, and the ability to experience passion and joy.

With substance addictions, physical health is impacted as well. Major organs like the liver, kidneys, and digestive systems can be impacted. Concurrently, imbalanced Sacred Core energy flow affects the well-being of the entire person.

Controlling behaviors attempt to compensate for lack of faith and self-confidence associated with the core chakra. Obsessive and controlling behaviors such as bullying, manipulation in relationships, or even self-isolation disrupt the potential for holistic creative, loving, and productive energy flow in the Sacred Core.

An obsessive need for heart centered oxytocin can manifest in patterns and cycles of codependent relationships. Creative vision, self-confidence, and passion and joy are disrupted when a person is engaged in abusive or unsupportive relationships.

Addictions and obsessions represent single dimensional attempts at fulfillment. Obsession related to any one energy center eventually restricts other sources of energy flow. At first, chemical and behavioral obsessions may make a person feel as if all energy flows are enhanced. Alcohol, opiates, stimulants, and hallucinogens (psychedelics) can produce ecstatic creative feelings. Obsessive behaviors may feel comforting and even exciting at first. Eventually, the energy centers and neuroreceptors associated with obsessions become fatigued and no longer provide the desired effects. With all other energy centers restricted, a great sense of emptiness can set in, as if no creative energy flows at all.

Human Limitations and Inspiration

While open flow of all energy centers would be ideal, human limitations also affect creative energy flow. Nobody has perfect multidimensional energy flow all the time. Everyone has baggage that bothers, distracts, and impedes reaching any absolute physical, spiritual, emotional, relationship, and creative potential.

The good news is that human limitations can also serve as motivators. When interpreted from a productive rather than from an obsessive and consumptive perspective, limitations can provide inspiration. For example, a child who is raised by addicts can be inspired to become an addiction therapist. Similarly, a victim of abuse from a codependent relationship can be inspired to become a productive advocate for other victims of abuse. Persons who manage and overcome limitations can be sources of inspiration for other people suffering similar challenges.

Productive reaction to challenges produces creative energy that helps self and others, and brings healing. Consumptive reactions sap energy from self and others and bring suffering. Positive energy produces positive, creative, and productive reactions and relationships. Negative energy depletes people and their relationships, and motivates consumptive reactions.

Positive and negative or productive and consumptive energy flow can also be associated with internal situational identities. For example, an addict may recognize a distinct "addictive personality" emerging when triggered or exposed to a substance of choice. A person with codependent tendencies stemming from obsession with heart centered energies may also recognize a "codependent identity" emerging when engaged in a relationship. The addictive or codependent identities or personalities may remain quite hidden while engaging in work or parenting activities, but emerge when presented an enabling environment or opportunity.

With mindful self-awareness, negative or consumptive identities can be recognized and accepted with compassion. Negative identities can eventually provide motivation for compassionate connection with others facing similar challenges.

With effort and support, eventually a person's Sacred Core can become a dominant identity. When protection identities rise up out of fear or obsession, Sacred Core in communion with Divine Other can provide a stabilizing and reassuring presence.

Sacred Core recognizes sacred self-worth, and reacts accordingly. For example, when a person engaged in a codependent relationship recognizes sacred self-worth, the internal identity that seeks out codependent relationships can be accepted with compassion. Steps can be taken to engage in self-care activities that intentionally exercise other energy centers. Healthy boundaries can be established (which are discussed in future chapters), and outside supportive relationships can be cultivated and engaged. Creative gifts can be developed and shared with others. A vision can develop for a life that includes creative engagement and healthy relationships. Self-confidence can grow and joy can be freely experienced.

Exercise:

The exercise for this section explores what characteristics Sacred Core identity can bring to each level of consciousness. With the outermost waking consciousness layer in mind, consider these questions. Jot down the first answers that come to mind.

1. When Sacred Core is an active and dominant identity, what kind of thoughts may occur in waking consciousness?

2. When Sacred Core is an active and dominant identity, what kinds of emotions might be felt during a normal day?

3. How may faith in self and Divine Other shape a person's activities and interactions with others?

4. What kinds of activities inspire passion and joy?

Similar questions can be considered at the subconscious level of consciousness, where situational identities reside:

1. What creative potential and gifts might Sacred Cores reveal within self?

2. How might Sacred Core express love toward situational identities?

3. How might Sacred Core identity encourage self-confidence?

4. How might Sacred Core interact with obsessive identities?

Finally, with the instinct level of consciousness in mind, consider these questions:

1. What kinds of automatic thoughts might Sacred Core encounter from the instinct level of consciousness?

2. How might Sacred Core interpret feelings of anger? Fear? Guilt or shame? Loneliness and longing?

3. How does Sacred Core interpret protective identities that respond with strong emotions?

4. What kinds of impulsive responses might Sacred Core encounter?

As always, this exercise is meant to build mindfulness and promote healing. Consider processing this exercise with a trusted person, whether friend, guide, or therapist. If the exercise evokes strong or painful emotions, set it aside and move on. The number one rule continues to be kindness toward self.

Consciousness Energy Flow

The practice in this chapter imagines sacred core energies expanding outward into the consciousness layers. As sacred core energies of creative vision, love, self-confidence, and joy move into the instinct layer, corresponding neurochemicals flow. Naturally occurring Endocannabinoids, Dopamine, Oxytocin, Serotonin, and Endorphins circulate throughout the nervous system.

In the instinct layer, feelings associated with survival are soothed and placated. Situations that may provoke involuntary fight or flight reactions are instead met with intentional actions. Supportive resources are engaged to ease long present fears and suffering.

In the subconscious, Sacred Core identity develops positive feelings. Vision develops for cultivating and sharing creative gifts. Creative projects and activities are undertaken. Healthy relationships are cultivated, and love and compassion for self and others grows. Self-confidence and a "can do" attitude develops, and set backs are met with understanding and resolve. Passion and joy are experienced in intimate relationships and in celebrating the creative accomplishments of self and others.

In the waking consciousness, thoughts become generally positive and hopeful. Relationships are warm and mutually supportive, supported by feelings of love. Challenges are met with a sense of acceptance and resilience. Thoughts tend to be productive and positive, supported by a sense of self confidence. Joyful experiences are simply accepted and enjoyed, aware of but not controlled by underlying obsessions or desires to prolong or intensify those experiences. Life goes on in a positive, productive manner.

Human challenges, whether physical, emotional, or spiritual and existential in nature, are generally accepted with compassion and self-care. People with medical and physical challenges engage in necessary self-care activities. People in recovery attend meetings and engage support as needed. People with long term mental health issues maintain the necessary medication and therapeutic regimens. Existential challenges like loneliness and loss are met with patience and compassion.

Best of all, people who become self-aware, and acknowledge, and accept their human limitations, can use their experience and wisdom to help others who endure similar human challenges.

Practice:

Thus far, practices have helped develop self-awareness with a goal of providing some relief from suffering. Feelings of self-confidence, love, joy, and clarity have been cultivated. Recognition of the human condition has been used to cultivate patience and compassion for self. A foundation has been set for evolving from consumptive obsessions that seek control, to productive acceptance that moves forward and learns and grows.

This is the eighth practice in the program. When viewed in its entirety, the practice reveals a rhythm of its own with contraction and expansion, emptying and fulfilling. The rhythm of the practice is like breathing. In this practice, the rhythm continues with the expansion of Sacred Self in communion with Divine Other into the layers of consciousness.

Like breathing, the earlier practices are beginning to feel familiar and natural. As you sit in a comfortable upright position, your breath is centered in your diaphragm. Your breath slows and deepens as you relax. You briefly recognize external and internal distractions, which you accept and release.

As easily as breathing, you begin the process of releasing layers of consciousness. With every breath a layer is released. Your waking consciousness, subconscious, and instinct layers are released. Rest for a moment in your sacred core, enjoying the Divine Life Ruach and Divine Consciousness Nephesh breezes flowing through your chakras.

Moving attention to your chakra energy centers, with each breath release negative energies. The mind chakra releases confusion. The heart chakra releases attachments and resentments. The core chakra releases aversions and fears. Finally, the root chakra releases obsessions and guilt.

Rest for a moment in this empty, peaceful space. Notice and accept the light and sound waves that seem to pass right through you. Your awareness is open, unhindered by internal distractions.

Recognize the presence of Divine Other within and all around you. Sacred Breath, Sacred Breeze, Sacred Spirit moves with every breath you take. Invite Divine Other to bring peace to your mind, love to your heart, peace and patience to your core, and joyful motivation to your root chakra.

Now quietly, peacefully, recognize your Divine Self rising. With every breath, sacred energy rises. You feel warmth as your root chakra energizes motivation. The warmth moves up to the core chakra, where you feel strength and confidence growing. Your heart glows with love and a sense of purpose. And your mind opens to creative clarity.

Take a moment and rest here, breathing and relaxed. Recognize the presence of Divine self in nondual communion with Divine Other. Recognize the flow of Sacred Breeze Energy throughout your core.

Now, slowly and gently, imagine Divine Self expanding to fulfill your instinct layer of consciousness. Imagine the concurrent flow of neurotransmitters, manifesting the Divine chakra energies in your physical body. Like Sacred Breeze energy, neurotransmitters release EDOSE energies throughout your body.

Breathing, imagine the mind chakra expanding and stimulating creative imagination, clarity, and optimism. Rest here in your mind for a moment, breathing. With every breath a sense of limitless possibility grows. With every breath, natural dopamine flows, and hopefulness abounds. Remain here for several breaths.

Move your attention to your heart chakra. Breathe. With every breath, love energy flows, stimulating the release of oxytocin. With every breath, love abounds. Unconditional and limitless, you feel growing compassion for self and others. Love from Divine Other courses through your body and shines outward. Remain here for several breaths.

Your attention moves down to your core chakra. Relax and notice your breath. With every breath, faith and self-confidence expands into your core nerve center. You are filled with a sense of peace and gratitude. With every breath, natural serotonin flows, and the wisdom that comes from experience and acceptance is recognized. Faith in self and faith in Other abounds. Remain here for several breaths.

Now move attention to your root chakra. Breathe. Notice the sensation and the rhythm of breathing. With every breath, natural endorphins flow, and a sensation of joy and enthusiasm grows. This sensation flows throughout your body. The feelings of joy and enthusiasm join the flowing energies of faith, love, and hope. Every breath brings a sense of fulfillment. Rest here, breathing, for several breaths.

Now, imagine your Sacred Core energy expanding into your subconscious. Relax and breath. With every breath, recognize some of the identities that are a part of you. Recognize the emotions that these identities carry with them. Some identities are productive, developing and sharing creative energy, and others are consumptive, needing care and attention. With every breath, acceptance is offered. With every breath, compassion abounds.

Human emotions are recognized, both positive and negative. Confusion is met with reassurance. Resentments are met with love. Fears, and obsessions that rise up to confront fears, are met with reassuring presence. With every breath, simply be present. Allow the presence of hope, faith, love, and joy to be experienced. Rest here for several breaths.

Allow your Sacred Core energy to expand once again, into waking consciousness. Emotions are accompanied by thoughts. With every breath, thoughts are recognized and accepted. Creative and hopeful thoughts exist side by side with confusion. Both are accepted and met with compassion. Breathe.

Loving thoughts exist side by side with neediness and resentments. Calming presence breathes, and, with every breath, offers understanding and compassion. Human and Divine, Flesh and Spirit, a knowing sense of I Am simply exists.

Thoughts of faith in self and faith in Divine Other arise. Faithful thoughts exist side by side with fears and doubts. Every breath brings awareness of reassuring presence. Acceptance and compassion abound. Every breath brings peaceful reassurance.

Joyful and enthusiastic thoughts exist side by side with obsessive thoughts. With every breath, both thoughts are accepted with compassion and understanding. This is full participation in human existence. Fears and doubts coexist with faith and hope. Resentments and obsessions coexist with love and joy. Neediness is met with compassion. Sacred Core Self recognizes the reality of existence and offers presence, compassion, and motivation to develop and share creativity for the benefit of self and others. A sense of wholeness emerges.

Return attention to your breath, resting in this feeling of wholeness. Allow gratitude to emerge. Gratitude for the gift of life. Gratitude for the gift of consciousness. Gratitude for Divine Inspiration and material existence.

Allow gratitude to expand to include your immediate environment. Allow positive feelings and intentions to grow for self and others. Positive regard is directed toward neighbors and the local town. Positive regard extends to animals, plants, and creatures in the local streams and lakes. Positive regard expands to include the local county, state, and province. Positive regard expands to include your country, continent, and the world. With gratitude, slowly emerge from your meditation.

9 AUTHENTIC, LOVING RELATIONSHIPS

In the last chapter, a holistic consciousness model is introduced. Sacred Core is described as a unified center of self, existing in relationship with protective and situational identities. Addiction is described as obsessive focus on individual chakra energy centers that neglect holistic energy flow. Finally, human limitations are discussed as sources of motivation and inspiration. In the practice, Sacred Core identity is expanded into all layers of consciousness.

The guiding principle for this program has been development and sharing creative gifts for the benefit of self and others. Sharing creative gifts can provide means and method for expressing love, reducing suffering, and providing service. The cultivation of healthy relationships is important for both the development and the sharing of creative gifts.

In this chapter, the consciousness plane is expanded into a relationship plane. Awareness of internal expectations and biases that affect relationships are explored. Energy flow and characteristics of healthy loving relationships are discussed. Codependent relationships, restorative Spiritual energy, and healthy Spiritual archetypes are also explored.

Narrative:

How had the marriage gone so wrong so quickly? He thought about how exciting and fun the relationship had been at first, including the dating, the parties, and the adventures they shared. He also remembered how interested he had been in her creative endeavors, as an artist and as a humanitarian. She appreciated his work as a teacher as well. She had expressed how impressed she was with his knowledge of history and his ability to connect with students. It was hard to believe that such an ideal partner, and such an ideal relationship, were possible.

The troubles began soon after the honeymoon, when "normal life" took over. In his mind, she wanted to continue to "play," with what seemed like a continuous stream of parties and commitments to her client galleries and political affiliations. Even worse, she seemed to care less whether he participated with her or not; she was perfectly happy to leave him at home while she went "galivanting about." As much fun as the honeymoon had been, this ongoing independent lifestyle didn't feel "normal" to him.

He considered how close his own family had been as he was growing up. Dad came home from work and they had dinner together most nights. The family often enjoyed game nights and movie nights together. As he got older, the interest his parents took in his relationships with friends and especially girlfriends seemed invasive, but for them being very close was normal. When he finally moved away from home, he felt relieved, able to breathe and find his own way, but at times he missed the closeness of his childhood.

Then he considered how very different her family of origin was. With her mom and dad both being working professionals, they hardly ever had meals together. Their interactions were quick, efficient, and somewhat impersonal in his view. At the time, having left what seemed like a smothering environment, their open and easy-going mannerisms seemed appealing.

He recalled how she had said over and over how "smothering" his expectations felt to her, and he expressed how lonely the relationship felt for him. He smiled at the irony of their circumstances. They were both drawn to opposite family lives, but their "family of origin" experiences took over.

When they first met, he had no expectations about the relationship with her. He loved her free-wheeling attitude and sometimes off-the-wall creativity. She took him places he never thought he would experience, on so many different levels.

It was then he decided, come what may, he would love and respect her for who she was, and try to be mindful when his expectations became oppressive to her. He realized he would have to accept himself as well, and engage in self-care for his own well-being. Maybe there was hope after all.

Relationship Plane

The exploration of relationships requires expanding the consciousness model outside of self. To expand the model outside of self, the relationship plane is introduced.

In previous chapters, consciousness was modeled with concentric rings. The various layers represent aspects of self, including conscious waking thoughts, subconscious feelings, and neurochemical instincts.

Physical Boundary
Waking Consciousness
Subconsciousness
Neurochemical - Instinct
Sacred Core

Figure 11: Consciousness Model

The relationship plane is represented in concentric rings as well, with each ring representing relationships as they exist in proximity to self:

Awareness Boundary
Unacquainted Others
Acquaintances
Family / Friends
Intimate Partner
Self

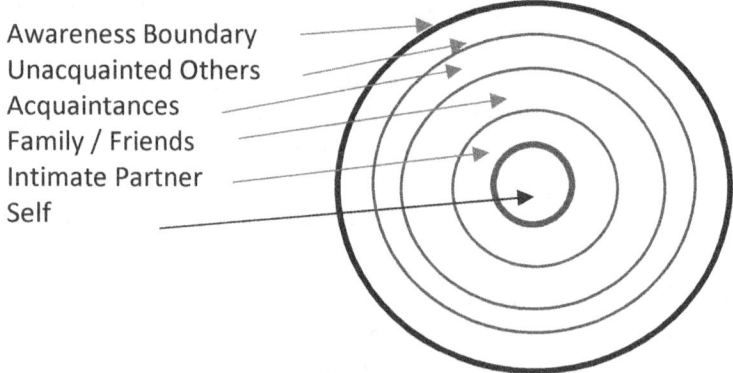

Figure 12: Relationships Consciousness Plane

In the relationship plane, the central "self" contains all the concentric layers of the consciousness plane. Layers outside the "self" represent "others", and the connections made between "self" and "others" are relationships.

Outside of the physical "self" boundary, the closest relationship is often with an intimate partner. Although there is a clear physical boundary between "self" and "other," the demarcation between self and other can be blurred in intimate relationships. The act of physical intimacy itself blurs the physical boundary, and corresponding cognitive, emotional, and even spiritual boundaries can become blurred as well.

When viewed from the instinct layer of consciousness, bonding occurs when both partners experiencing sympathetic flows of neurochemicals. Shared experiences, including sex, sleeping together, and interacting with others result in mutual sympathetic flows of oxytocin, endorphins, serotonin, dopamine, and endocannabinoids. The sympathetic flow of neurochemicals is perceived as "feeling the same things at the same time." With such intimate sharing of deep instinct level feelings, the blurring of the line between self and other is understandable.

Outside of intimacy, the next layer in the relationship plane represents close familial relationships, including relationships with children, parents, and very close friends. Depending on the age and closeness of the people in very close relationships, demarcations between self and other can also become blurred. Shared activities and shared history can create an environment in which sympathetic neurochemical flow occurs as well. For example, when people enjoy a meal together, everyone simultaneously experiences the flow of neurochemicals that create a sense of relaxed enjoyment.

The next layer in the relationships model includes friends and work associates. At this level social norms and boundaries reinforce a clear demarcation between self and others. Internal situational identities emerge to guide behaviors and relationships. Cooperation becomes a prominent feature of these relationships, and the focus moves from communal sharing toward achieving common goals. Relationships at this layer may also include teachers, students, clients, and customers. These relationships are usually less intimate and require professional boundaries and decorum.

The next layer outside of friends and professional relationships are casual acquaintances, which involve people who are encountered during day-to-day activities such as marketplace exchanges and walking in public. At this level, faces and names become less and less familiar when compared to closer relationships.

Object Relationships

While relationships are most noticeably formed with people and living creatures such as pets, relationships are formed with objects as well. Perhaps the closest object relationship exists with tools of a trade or artistic expression. Examples of close relationship objects include musical instruments, computers and cell phones, carpentry tools, oil paints and canvas, machinery, and land worked by gardeners and farmers. Anyone who has negotiated currents and winds in a boat, has mixed colors and applied layers of paint to a canvas, or blended layers of sound in a musical composition, understands that the use of tools becomes second nature. Tools become an extension of a person.

From the object point of view, the next layer out might include domestic items that help someone feel comfortable and safe. Examples include a home or apartment, a garden, or a favorite alcove or studio where one spends time reading and being creative.

Object relationships in the furthest layers out may include objects that are observed and enjoyed but not owned. Examples include paintings in museums, sunsets, and objects admired while browsing or shopping.

Of course, there is a major difference between object relationships and relationships with people and living creatures. While objects can serve as extensions of self, living creatures and people are sacred and autonomous each in their own right.

For a carpenter, a hammer may feel and act like an extension of self. Similarly, a spouse may also feel like an extension of self, especially if the relationship is very entangled and boundaries are not clear. But the fact remains that both parties in a living relationship are autonomous beings, each sacred and individual in his and her own right. Conflicts often arise when people start "taking each other for granted" and using each other as if they were objects without regard for sacred autonomy.

In describing the difference between object and person relationships, the Jewish philosopher Martin Buber famously describes the differences between "I-It" relationships and "I-You" relationships in his book "I and Thou." (Buber, 1923/1996)

Awareness Boundary

At the far end of the relationship spectrum is another physical boundary or horizon beyond which lies unknown people and objects. Beyond that boundary, a person has no awareness of the existence or non-existence of people, places, and things.

Fortunately, because humans are curious and intelligent beings, the awareness boundary is always expanding. With education, travel, new work environments and experiences, and meeting new people, the relationship awareness boundary is always expanding.

While the external awareness boundary can be related to physically distant people, places, and things, the boundary can also be physically quite close. Microscopic, atomic, and subatomic objects are undetectable without the benefits of education and specialized instruments for observation. For example, until a person learns about the biological workings of the human body, the existence of organs and cells and antibodies exist outside the boundary of awareness.

Just as there is an awareness boundary with the external universe, there is also an awareness boundary within the internal universe. For the most part people are unaware of what is going on inside the subconsciousness. Hints can be discerned from dreams and emotions, but for most people the workings of the subconscious remain a mystery. Similarly, people are unaware of the deep instinctual / neurological universe. Hints can be found from observing automatic reactions (like pulling a hand away from a hot object), but for the most part the instinct operates autonomously and anonymously. An even greater mystery is the transcendent core, with a still small voice that can supersede even the basest of instincts and provide motivation to challenge long held beliefs and behaviors.

While new experiences like education and travel expand the external boundary, mindfulness practices like meditation expand the inner boundaries. With introspection, awareness of personal strengths and limitations grows, as does awareness of the inner forces that provide motivation and restraint. Some of the inner forces include the multiple situational identities that have been discussed. While situational identities represent models or archetypes for behavior in different contexts, sacred Core identity represents the sacred "I Am" locus of who a person is.

Relationship Model

Consider the following graphical representation of relationship:

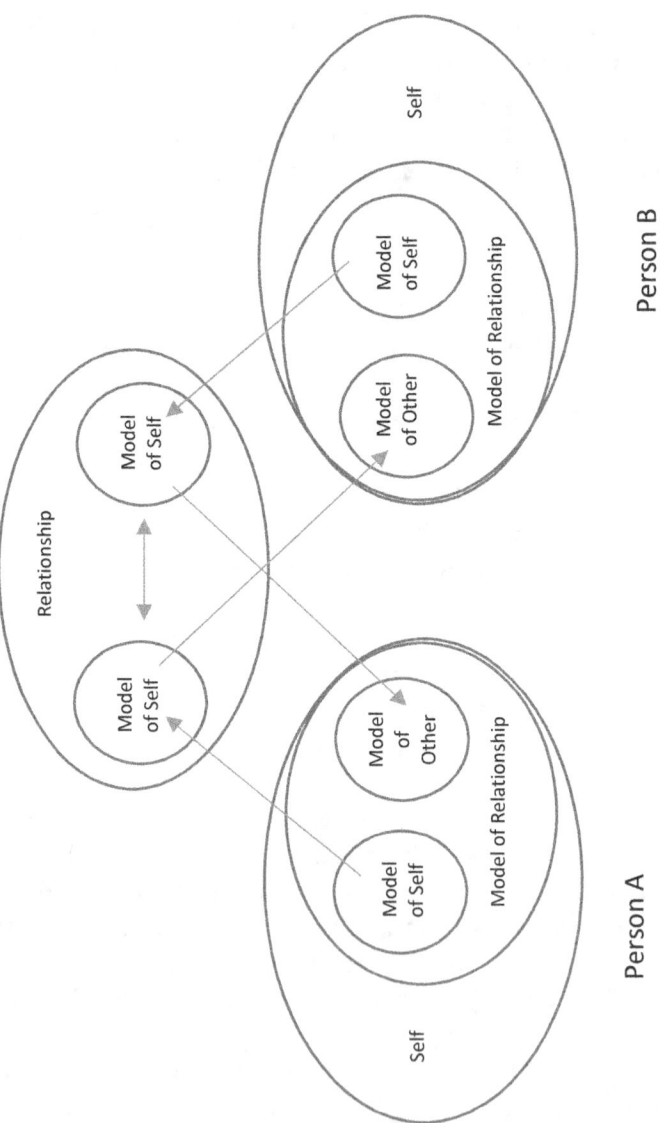

Figure 13: Relationship Model

In the illustration, person A holds within his or her consciousness an archetypal model for self (or identity) in relationship, an archetypal model for the other in relationship, and an archetypal model for the relationship itself. Person B has the same internal models or archetypes of self, person A, and the relationship. The actual relationship is the place where the internal representations of self are shared with the other.

Notice that the experience of "other" in a relationship is filtered through two models, the model of self that the other presents to the relationship and the model of other that self carries within.

Outside of the relationship, both person A and person B are autonomous sacred beings. Every sacred being represents a unique universe of consciousness. The depth and breadth of each consciousness represents a mystery even to the self.

The relationship diagram clearly illustrates the challenges of getting to authentically know someone else in a relationship. Both parties carry multiple filters and expectations, and both parties represent an entire universe of sacred consciousness and mystery.

The model of the self that is shared with others is usually controlled by a situational identity, depending on the context of the relationship. As contexts change in the relationship, the situational identity presented to the relationship changes as well. For example, a spouse working on the family taxes thinks and behaves differently from the same spouse participating in an intimate dinner for two. Similarly, a person participating in a social event with her or his family of origin may present a more child-like situational identity than the same person participating in a professional social event.

Archetypes of Other

As illustrated above, archetypes or models exist within the subconscious that represent others in relationships. Archetypes are similar to situational identities, but rather than representing self, they represent others. For example, an archetype of "mother" or "father" can exist in a person's subconscious quite independently from a person's actual parent.

To some extent, a person's satisfaction with a relationship depends on how closely the actual person in the relationship matches the internal archetype. For example, if "mom" or "dad" doesn't live up to the expectations one carries for a "good mother" or "good father," a level of dissatisfaction and conflict can arise in the relationship.

These models or archetypes of others extend to all external relationships, living and object. Everyone carries archetypes representing what it means for a spouse, a parent, or a hammer or a paintbrush to be "good" in relationship.

Relationship Archetypes

In addition to archetypes for self and others, people carry models for what they believe good relationships are like. Examples might include an idealized family, an idealized marriage, and an idealized provider-customer relationship.

Notice in the diagram that relationship itself is represented as a third party, independent of person A and person B. A relationship takes on unique characteristic different from how each participant models the relationship. Relationships can actually be considered third parties, independent from either of the persons in the relationship.

As an example of "relationship as third party." consider a relationship that includes physical intimacy. When a relationship involves physical intimacy, the relationship can manifest into a separate "third party" physical human being with the conception of a child.

Just as people carry models or archetypes for others (ideal spouse, ideal parent, ideal doctor, etc.), people carry models or archetypes for relationships. In business, contracts are often used to specify relationship archetypes so that all parties in the relationship are aware of expectations and boundaries.

While intimate relationships can be formalized with legal marriage contracts, the workings of the relationship archetypes that each partner carries into relationships are difficult to define. When the relationship, as a third party, looks different than either party expects, there can be conflict.

Like models for people, the models for relationships also are based on experience and societal influences. For example, a child raised in a family where the physical, emotional, and spiritual demarcations or boundaries between "self" and "other" are not clearly defined would consider tightly entangled relationships normal. Such relationships can be very close and very dependent. In tightly entangled relationships most activities are shared, and participating in groups or activities outside the entangled relationship is less prevalent.

Another child raised by two working parents with little time for family interaction would consider highly independent relationships normal. In such relationships, shared activities such as meals or vacations might be very rare, while participation in independent activities outside the home would be much more prevalent.

Households in which family members cooperate interactively and have some degree of independence to develop creative gifts and friendships outside the immediate family provide an interdependent relationship model. Interdependent relationships are characterized by cooperation, mutual support, and respect for each other. Physical, intellectual, emotional, and spiritual boundaries are respected, and each party in the relationship continues to develop both independently and cooperatively.

Relationships in family of origin create the archetypes that influence a person's view of what "normal" relationships looks like. Sometimes family of origin archetypes are challenged or even rejected during adolescent development or later in life. Whether the family influences are accepted or rejected, the influence of childhood formed archetypes are carried into relationships outside the family of origin and into intimate, friendship, and even working relationships later in life.

Relationships and Energy Flow

Relationships are often characterized in terms of giving and receiving. For example, in a parent-child relationship or a doctor-patient relationship, an expectation is set that the parent or doctor provides care and service, while the child or patient receives the care or service.

While the relationship plane provides a model for connecting with people outside self, another way to look at the relationship plane is in terms of energy flow.

Dependent relationships often require a great deal of outward energy flow on everyone's part. Examples of dependent relationships include jobs where employee activities are micro-managed, or families where everyone's activities are closely monitored.

Independent relationships may require little energy flow, but also may lack in emotional connection. Examples of independent relationships include jobs where very little direction is given, or families that are so busy with outside activities they rarely interact with each other.

Interdependent relationships are characterized by energy flow that goes both ways. Sharing responsibilities and caring and supporting one another can create a satisfying, reciprocal energy flow for everyone, in employment or family environments. A mutual flow of energy strengthens both the relationships and the individuals in the relationship.

Codependent Relationships

Relationships that include demanding, dominant, or needy personalities are considered codependent. Such relationships require a great deal of energy that is difficult and often impossible to maintain.

Codependent relationships can play out in a repeated cycle that is increasingly abusive. An abusive cycle is characterized by conflict or abuse, followed by a honeymoon period, followed by increased tension, and then a repeat of conflict or abuse.

Individuals in relationships can exchange roles as part of the cycle. Codependency can manifest as a dance in which partners exchange roles as submissive and dominant.

People raised in codependent environments form internal relationship archetypes that seek out codependent individuals. If the internal model that a person holds for relationship is characterized by a constant single direction giving or taking of energy, the person will seek out other persons that fit the model. This is why persons who leave one abusive relationship often find themselves in another abusive relationship.

As described in previous chapters, codependent relationships can be considered a form of addiction.

Restorative Spiritual Energy

Energy flow in relationships can also be described as "Spiritual energy." Living creatures have the capacity to produce, share, and consume spiritual energy in relationship with others.

As discussed in Chapter 5, living creatures also have access to Spiritual energy sourced from within the Sacred Core. Sacred core has the capacity to recognize and accept restorative life energy and consciousness energy through mindful practices like meditation and prayer. Internal energy resources can bolster self-confidence and strength during trying times. Spiritual energy sourced from one's Sacred Core can bring awareness of challenging and addictive internal archetypes that make healthy relationships difficult to form and maintain. Sacred Core energy encourages healing.

Restorative energy can be found from external sources as well. For example, restorative energy can be found in communal worship, in cooperation, and in charitable activities. Examples of restorative external resources include mutually supportive groups like Alcoholics Anonymous, Narcotics Anonymous, and grief recovery groups.

Restorative energy can also be discerned from mindfully recognizing and enjoying nature. Sunshine, fresh air, beaches and walks in gardens and forests can provide a great deal of restorative energy.

Everyone needs resources for restorative Spiritual energy. Life itself consumes energy. Restorative Spiritual energy can help a person through energy consuming conditions like illness, aging, and loss.

Even healthy relationships require additional energy for maintenance, because no relationship is perfect. The task of adjusting internal expectations and archetypes as a way of authentically connecting with others can be taxing. Internal and external spiritual energy resources can help with meeting the challenges of both the human condition and relationships.

Spiritual Archetypes

For some people, internal spiritual resources can feel draining rather than restorative. Traditions and cultures that cultivate shame and fear or archetypes of angry and vengeful gods can create a constant drain on a person's energy. When a person experiences such a constant internal drain on spiritual energy, external relationships suffer as well.

Spiritual interpretations and relationships that demand energy from self and others are not healthy. Authentic core self is aware of the cost of unhealthy spiritual interpretations and relationships. The still small voice from within recognizes the presence or absence of spiritual fruits like love, peace, patience, and kindness. Even if a person is not familiar with the presence or existence of Spiritual gifts and fruits, the still small voice from within has the ability to both share and receive those fruits.

The sharing of Spiritual fruits manifests in the cultivation and sharing of creative gifts in healthy exchanges of spiritual energy. With healthy internal spirituality and healthy external relationships, creative gifts can be shared for the benefit of self and others.

Exercise: Relationship Archetypes

As an exercise in raising self-awareness, consider your own attitudes regarding "ideal relationships."

- What does an ideal spouse look like? What expectations does this create?
- What does an ideal mother or father look like? What expectations does this create?
- What does an ideal friendship look like? An ideal marriage or partnership?
- How do these expectations affect your relationships? How do they affect authentically knowing another person?
- How would you characterize your family of origin relationships? Dependent, Independent, Codependent, or Interdependent?
- How does your family of origin experience affect your current relationships?
- How would you characterize your relationship with Divine Other? Is the idea of Divine Other demanding and draining, or loving and encouraging?
- How does your understanding of Divine Other affect your external relationships?

Practice: Mindful Relationships

Awareness of energy flow is important for cultivating healthy relationships. Meditation practices in previous chapters have focused on recognizing healthy positive energy flow from internal Spiritual resources. In this chapter's practice, the focus is on recognizing energy flow in relationships. There is also an emphasis on recognizing archetypes and expectations that influence relationships.

The practice begins with a comfortable and upright posture. Begin to breathe using your diaphragm and recognize the feel of your stomach rising and falling with each breath.

At this point, you should be very familiar with the process of breathing, letting go of distractions, and receiving inspiration. The previous practices can be experienced as preparation using a single breath for each step in the process.

Picture your layers of consciousness. Breathe, and imagine releasing your waking consciousness. Take another breath, and release your subconscious feelings. With another breath, release your deep instinctual feelings.

Step inside your sacred core and breathe. Using your diaphragm, inhale and recognize the flow of consciousness energy through your mind, your heart, your core, and your root. Now exhale and recognize external life energy flowing through your root, your core, your heart, and your mind. Visualize this flow of energy with every breath, mind to root, and root to mind, inhale, and exhale.

After several breaths, move your attention into your mind chakra. Allow a cleansing inhale to sweep into your mind, and with an exhale release any confusing thoughts. Moving your attention to your heart chakra, allow an inhale to sweep into your heart, and with an exhale release any attachments. Moving attention to your core chakra, allow an inhale to sweep into your core, and with an exhale release any fears and aversions. Finally, move your attention to your root chakra. Allow an inhale to sweep into your root, and with an exhale release any obsessions.

Recognize the sense of inner cleansing that comes with self-emptying. Rest in the emptiness for a moment, breathing. Open your awareness to your surrounding environment, physically and spiritually. Sounds and feelings, light and energy drift and flow through your body, as if you are transparent. With every breath, enjoy the sensation of unattached freedom.

From this state of emptiness, inhale and allow a nondual communion of sacred self and Other to rise into the root chakra. Allow feelings of motivation and joy to emerge. Breathe again and move to the core, allowing feelings of faith and confidence to rise up. Moving to the heart, breathe again and allow feelings of unconditional acceptance and love to emerge. With one more breath, allow your mind chakra to experience clarity and freedom. Breathe and experience a sense of wholeness, and with every breath allow sacred energy to flow.

Prepare your sacred core self to expand back into your layers of consciousness. Breathe and expand sacred core into your instinct layer of consciousness. Allow sacred energy to flow. Allow acceptance and love for your protector identities. Breathe again and expand into the subconscious. With every breath, experience soothing and reassuring Sacred Core energy touching your situational identities with acceptance and love. Finally, breathe and expand into waking consciousness. Allow peace and joy to flow along with a sense of hope and clarity.

Take a moment to just rest here. This is the launching point into your journey outside of self. With a relaxed breath, imagine your consciousness expanding outward beyond the boundary of your skin. Recognize your very close and intimate relationships. With every breath, observe the feelings that arise. If you find yourself reacting to those feelings, breathe through them. Remember your breath is your refuge, your safe space. Simply observe the feelings as they arise, and breathe through them. As you consider very close and intimate relationships, you may experience emotions. There may be love. There may be frustration. There may be joy, or even anger. Whatever feelings arise, recognize and breathe through them. Accept your feelings without judgment and continue to breathe. The feelings you experience provide information that affects how you experience relationships. Try to not process; just observe and release.

Expand your consciousness to include close friends and family. Recognize that the feelings that arise are sourced from your own internal archetypes and expectations. Recognize these expectations come from family of origin experience and society. Intimate relationship archetypes and expectations directly affect energy flow in relationships.

When you think of very close and intimate relationships, recognize any sense of vacuum or need you feel that wants to pull energy from them. Recognize any desire for control that might push or impose energy on others. Recognize warm feelings that create a satisfying exchange of energy flow. With each breath, become familiar with the flow of energy between you and these very close relationships. Without judgment, recognize these feelings and breathe. There is no judgment here, only observation.

Take a moment to relax and release. Find refuge in your breath, before moving to the next layer. Cleanse yourself of the feelings and thoughts you just experienced. Move your consciousness outward, recognizing friend and coworker relationships. With every breath, recognize your feelings as they arise. Recognize feelings of satisfaction, frustration, or worry. Recognize the energy you provide that helps bring fulfillment to them. Recognize the energy you receive that helps bring fulfillment to you. With every breathe, recognize and release these thoughts and feelings.

Consider the models and expectations shape your experience of feelings. Expectations include giving and receiving of care in relationships, and simply being available and present. Try to not judge;

just recognize, accept, and release.

Take a moment to breathe and relax, releasing your thoughts and experiences from the friend and coworker layer. Now expand your consciousness to include casual acquaintances. Recognize your feelings when you encounter others during casual circumstances. Introverts tend to feel drained and even threatened when they experience casual encounters. Extroverts tend to feel energized and hopeful. Some casual relationships can create a motivation for becoming closer as friends.

Recognize that these feelings also arise from internal archetypes. Your feelings and expectations arise from your culture and experience. Recognize that the reality of casual encounters may be very different from your expectations, as is the case with all relationships.

Consider the energy flow in casual relationships. A sense of obligation to fix or control casual relationships may be draining. Feelings of suspicion or expectations of requiring service may be experienced as draining to others. A mutual exchange of friendly greeting may feel uplifting to both self and other in any encounter.

Now take a moment to release all thoughts and feelings. Take several cleansing breaths, recognizing your moving diaphragm.

Imagine yourself standing on the edge of your awareness. Imagine gazing out into the vast space that is the unknown. Recognize the feelings you experience. For some, this can feel frightening and threatening. For others, this can feel exciting and adventurous. Energy may be flowing outward in hope and expectation, or inward in retreat and fear.

"Unknown" archetypes may be the most powerful of all. The expectations you have about encountering the unknown come from your culture and experiences. There is no judgment here; there is only information. If you are comfortable, allow your imagination to rest here, gazing out over the vast unknown. If you are uncomfortable focus on your breathing, which is your safe refuge. Relax and breathe.

Finally, allow yourself to return to within the bounds of your own skin and consciousness. Breathe and relax. Energy flows from your internal resources, from Divine Consciousness and Divine Life energy. With every breath, experience healing and restoration. Accept these experiences with a sense of gratitude.

Allow yourself to feel positive intentions toward yourself. Consider the living people and creatures near you, within your home and immediate surroundings. Allow yourself to feel positive intentions toward them. Imagine the people and living creatures in your local neighborhood and town. Include plants, trees, fish in the streams, and animals. Breathe and extend positive intentions. Moving outward, allow yourself to feel positive intentions toward everyone in your state or province, and in your country. Finally, allow your positive intentions to extend to the entire world.

With one final cleansing breath, emerge from your meditation.

10 COMPASSION FOR OTHER

In the previous chapter, the external relationship plane is presented. Archetypes and expectations that represent both people and relationships are described as filters that challenge a person's ability to engage in authentic relationships. The concept of energy flow in relationships is also introduced. Relationships are described as healthy when spiritual energy flows in both directions rather than a constant flow of energy from one person toward another. Codependent relationships are described, and healthy relationship within the context of Spirituality were considered as well.

Whereas the previous chapter described the characteristics of healthy relationships that support the development and sharing of creativity, this chapter focuses on authenticity. When ego centered expectations are set aside, authentic, loving connection is possible. Authentic loving connection can happen through mutual commitment to accept one another, through shared creative expression, and through compassionate presence. Authentic loving connection represents the fulfillment of human potential for engaging in relationships that benefit self and others. The deepest and broadest feelings of satisfaction and fulfillment that a human can experience are possible through loving relationships.

Narrative

Her mother was dying, and there was nothing she could do about it. Despite being a medical doctor, she could do nothing. She felt powerless.

She prayed. And yet, the thought of it almost made her laugh. In her experience, God did not intervene. If God intervened, the Holocaust would never have happened. Countless earthquakes, tsunamis, and weather disasters that took away countless lives would never have happened. And her own skills as a physician would not be needed. In the context of all human sufferings, her prayers on behalf of her mother seemed arrogant and meaningless.

Her time as a working professional was always demanding; patients were lined up on schedule and she was compelled to rush from one to the next, spending precious little time with any individual. Her training and skills either helped her patients, or they did not. Most of her patients had the capacity to heal themselves, given a nudge in the right direction with medication or intervention of some kind. But not her mother. Her mother was terminal.

The last time she had been with her mother, she could almost feel the pain, despite the steady drip of narcotics. Still, when mom opened her eyes, a smile always followed. She asked her mother whether there was anything she could do to make her more comfortable. Her mother replied "you being here is enough."

But being with her mother was hard. Being with her mother reminded her of her own powerlessness before the existential realities of being human. She pursued a career in medicine to fight that sense of powerlessness. And yet, here she was. "We're ultimately alone, and we're going to die" she whispered to herself silently.

Her thoughts drifted back to what her mother had said. "You being here is enough." Simply being present with her mother helped ease the pain, the emptiness, and fear they both felt.

She thought again about her prayers. Though she felt anger toward God's "lack of intervention," she also recognized that when she let the anger go, when she opened herself to the experience, she felt comforted.

She thought again about her mother, lying helpless and in pain. A vision of her mother as a child came to mind, running through the forest preserve with cousins, playing on the beach. She saw her mother growing up, through awkward teenage years with a father who was so protective he sometimes seemed abusive. She saw her mother working, dating, and meeting her own father for the first time. Suddenly all her disappointments from her own childhood, times that her mother was not present, not supportive, not perfect, all slipped away. She saw her mother as the sacred, creative, beautiful girl and woman she had always been.

Sighing, she called her scheduling service and cleared her calendar. She would see patients in the mornings, but the afternoons she would spend with her mother. Just being present. Sometimes in silent prayer. Just her, her mom, and God.

Ego as Expectation

From the perspective of Buddhist philosophy, projected archetypes and expectations for self, others, and relationships originate within the ego. In Buddhism, ego-based expectations and desires are considered the root of all suffering. With the release of ego, authentic expression and connection between self and others is possible.

Most people are not aware of ego-based projections and expectations, which have been described previously as context based situational identities. Ego provides a subconscious process for engaging in relationships that can be both helpful and limiting.

Ego can help make casual interactions efficient. For example, a person buying a cup of coffee or a meal usually projects a polite, customer identity, while the person selling the coffee or meal projects a helpful, service-oriented identity. Communication and exchange occur, and both parties are happy. Authentic connection may occur during the exchange and through the creative care that goes into preparing the meal or the drink, but the exchange is made relatively easy through common expectation models. If both parties are genuinely polite and helpful without distraction, a simple connection can be authentic as well. Often, however, people are preoccupied by many other concerns while engaging in simple transactions. Without the expectation of simple exchange guiding the interaction, a simple "how are you today?" could turn into a long, involved process that interferes with the desired transaction.

Ego can also provide protection against potentially harmful relationships. When the dynamics of a relationship fall too far outside expected norms, discomfort arises which may result in the termination of the relationship. Termination may be beneficial, thereby preventing harm for either person. Using the previous example, an impolite customer or an unhelpful service person can disrupt a marketplace relationship so that an expected exchange of goods and services may not be completed. Termination may be preferable to an uneven exchange or escalation and conflict.

Ego as Prejudice

Not all ego centered expectations are helpful or healthy. Ego centered expectations can be a source of unfair prejudice. For example, a person with subconscious prejudiced ego expectations based on race, ethnicity, or sexual orientation might avoid relationships or even be abusive with people who carry those characteristics.

Whether based on prejudice or not, overly protective egos can impede the forming of healthy relationships. Egos that are predatory in nature can engage in unhealthy codependent relationships that demand energy from others. Egos that do not hold strong enough expectations can fall victim to predators that demand energy. Whether too rigid, too open, or predatory, unhealthy egos can interfere with creative development and sharing as well as with healthy intimacy.

Mindfulness practices, such as meditation, can help a person recognize and release ego-based prejudices, just as meditation can help a person release internal sources of suffering. Release of ego can free a person from the limitations associated with automatic subconscious reactions in relationships.

Authenticity, Acceptance, and Love

In the previous chapter, some effort is made to recognize, accept, and release ego-based expectations at every level of the relationship plane. Just as in prior chapters where internal identities are recognized, acceptance remains a key part of releasing expectations. Remember the relationship model shared in the previous chapter that described three layers of ego involved in relationships. Acceptance in relationships can be more difficult than accepting internal identities because expectations are imposed on self, other, and relationship itself.

Once expectations are acknowledged, the work of accepting true authentic self, other, and relationship begins. Acceptance of true self and other allows sharing of true self, and creates a safe space for others to share true self in kind. The goal of all this acceptance is authentic loving relationship.

While being an authentic person is a worthy goal, authenticity is also constrained by human limitations. Because every human being holds an entire universe of consciousness within, even the most mindful person has a limited view of the depths of sacred core self, sacred other, and all the situational identities that exist within the subconsciouses of self and other. Recognizing and accepting human limitations can always be a humbling experience.

When mutual love, respect, and compassion exist in authentic relationship, the process of sharing authentic selves with each other can provide a lifetime of companionship and discovery. The healthy interchange of spiritual energy that occurs in mutually loving relationships can inspire feelings of joy and fulfillment that transcend human limitations.

Healthy Boundaries

Ego based projections and expectations can subconsciously provide benefits, protection, and challenges. The protections subconsciously put in place by ego are also known as boundaries.

While subconsciously placed boundaries can provide protection, they can also be the source of unwarranted prejudice and rejection. Healthy intentional and conscious boundaries can provide an alternative to subconscious ego-based projections and expectations. Healthy boundaries are intentionally formed based on mindful awareness of self and other, rather than unintentional reaction from subconscious ego.

A boundary is a line that demarcates the border between self and other. While physical skin demarcates a physical boundary between self and other, a relationship boundary demarcates control of a person's body, how a person spends her/his time and resources, and how a person lives.

Boundaries are not mechanisms for controlling others. Boundaries are only useful for controlling self. Boundaries help a person to define what will and will not be tolerated in relationships with others. Once boundary definitions are made, a person is free to decide what to reveal and what to accept in relationships.

For example, if a person has a spouse or partner who "gets loud and close" during conversations, a boundary may be set to not tolerate such loud and controlling behaviors. Once the boundary is set, a person may communicate an intent to walk away when those conditions occur. Later when calm is restored, a conversation may be continued.

Boundaries can also be helpful in relationships that exist inside a person. Sacred core self coexists with internal situational identities or egos. Mindfulness coupled with boundaries can help a person recognize the influence internal identities have in external relationships. Being aware of the internal identities can help a person control unwanted behaviors.

Using the same example, the "loud and controlling" spouse may become aware of an internal identity that feels insecure during certain conversations and circumstances. When a feeling of insecurity is recognized, an internal boundary can be exercised. Sacred core self can provide reassurance to the insecure identity and consciously manage the external behavior. Recognizing the boundary may help an aggressive person to delay or walk away from an uncomfortable conversation.

People often make the error of believing that healthy boundaries can be imposed on others. Using the previous example, a person who does not fully understand boundaries might say, "I'm imposing a boundary that you aren't going to get loud or controlling during our conversations." The error in this statement is that boundaries do not control other people's behaviors; boundaries control only the behavior of self. Instead of saying, "Don't yell any more", a person with healthy boundaries may say "When you get loud, I'm going to walk away."

The same rules apply to internal relationships. Internal identities are established early in life and cannot simply be controlled. Trying to tell an internal identity "Do not get loud ever again" is unrealistic and just creates frustration. To mindfully recognize escalating emotions allows sacred core self to reassure an insecure internal identity and manage external behavior.

People in relationships can enlist help from each other to recognize difficult behaviors that rise up from within. For example, a person who tends to get loud during disagreements can request that a partner help with recognizing the behavior. The person requesting help might say, "Would you please let me know when my voice starts getting loud? I have trouble recognizing when this happens." The external help with recognition can help reinforce internal boundaries used to control behaviors.

While boundaries offer a useful tool for managing unhealthy behaviors, they also project healthy attributes of self-worth and self-esteem. A person who maintains healthy boundaries recognizes the sacred worth of self and others. With consciously established healthy boundaries in place, a person has the option and ability to recognize and release ego projections and expectations and share aspects of authentic self with others. People recognize authentic presence and authentic sharing. When encountering authentic sharing, other people often respond with authentic sharing in kind.

Authentic Self and Creativity

When ego-based expectations are released, authentic self can be exposed. Consequently, sharing authentic self can create a sense of vulnerability. One might remember a time during adolescence when presenting an identity that was "cool and confident" felt important in gaining acceptance from peers. In this example, exposing authentic self may require dropping an ego based "cool and confident" projection.

Sacred Core Divine Self in communion with Divine Other has awareness of and compassion for human vulnerability. All the practices described in previous chapters come together in sharing authentic self. The joy, self-confidence, love, and authenticity that emanate from Divine Self is by far more substantial than any ego-based projection of false confidence.

Authentic self also understands intentional boundaries. No longer subject to the whims of internal identities and ego for protection, authentic self can consciously choose what to share and with whom to share. When authentic self participates in casual relationships, context appropriate sharing takes place, but the sharing is intentional rather than automatically brought forth from the subconscious. When authentic self participates in close and intimate relationships, vulnerability can be intentionally and mutually shared for the benefit of both people.

Authentic self also shares through creative expression. Whether art, music, cooking, or direct caring or teaching relationships, the combination of developed skills and sharing authentic self can inspire others. When a person encounters an authentic presence through a creative work, an authentic connection is formed.

Sharing authentic self through creative expression risks vulnerability. Critique, rejection, or indifference to a person's creative product is possible. Sacred Core self provides the resilience and self-confidence to intentionally manage the risk.

Honest critique can help a person refine creative skills. One does not expect a child with crayons to produce Monet quality artwork immediately. With encouragement, maturation, and helpful critique, skills can be refined to the point at which a person's creative potential is realized. A mature and mindful Sacred Core has the ability to discern helpful and honest critique, and respond with practice and improvement over time.

When ego encounters indifference or rejection of a person's creative expression, an automatic reaction of hurt and even isolation can result. Experiencing indifference or rejection of one's creative work can be difficult, but a mature and mindful Sacred Core can allow a person to react with compassion and curiosity. Indifference or rejection may come from creative work not resonating with an audience, or resonating too closely with another person's inner identities. Either way, curiosity and compassion can help a creative person to understand the source of another person's reaction or indifference. Compassionate curiosity provides a path for conscious self-critique, which can also motivate a person to develop and refine artistic skills.

When authentic self connects with a creative work, inspiration is possible. Inspiration is a transfer of Spiritual energy that benefits both the source and the receiver of the creativity. The creative person receives benefit whether appreciation for the creative work is received or not. Creativity is the gift that keeps on giving. Creative expression can live on and inspire others long after an author or artist has passed on, as evidenced by poets and artists like Ovid, Cicero, Dickens, Mozart, Bowie, and Prince, whose creative works continue to inspire authentic connection between artist and audience. Creative caring can live on as well, shared from person to person, and even generation to generation.

Motivation for Creativity

Life includes experiences that inspire feelings of both suffering and joy. Authentic connections provide a means of sharing experiences and feelings of both suffering and joy with others. Sharing authentic experiences and feelings can inspire positive feelings that range from relief to fulfillment.

Developing a creative work is an act of expressing authentic self. Sharing creative work is an act of sharing authentic self. Creative work serves as the relationship through which an artist's authentic self is shared with others. The acts of creating and sharing authentic self can feel rewarding and fulfilling.

When an audience can relate to feelings of suffering and joy conveyed through creative expression, a connection is made. When a creative work resonates with another person, the authentic self of other connects with the authentic self of the artist. Even when suffering is conveyed through artistic expression, authentic connection inspires positive feelings. Realizing that feelings and experiences are shared, that one's suffering and joy are not experienced in isolation, brings comfort and affirmation.

Authentic connection through creative works can inspire others to also develop and pursue creative expression, forging more authentic connections and positive feelings with more people. The cascade of inspiration that can result from authentic creative sharing can span generations.

When a person experiences positive feelings of connection and inspiration, appreciation is sometimes expressed toward the artist. The expression of appreciation is also an act of sharing authentic experience and feeling. Authentic connection from audience to artist further motivates creative expression.

Creative Stagnation and Compassion

After some time, sharing through creative works may begin to feel redundant. Over time the experiences and feelings that motivate creative expression can seem to dissipate. When the need for creative expression dissipates, compassion for others can provide fresh motivation and inspiration.

Authentic sharing originates within Sacred Core Self. Sacred Core exists in communion with Divine Other. Sacred Core is motivated by love and compassion, to bring healing and reconciliation to self and others.

Authentic relationship also inspires love for others. When another person in an authentic relationship suffers, compassion emerges. Compassion provides motivation to help relieve suffering that others experience. (Lopez et al, 2018)

For example, a blues musician may be motivated to share challenging experiences and feelings through music. People who appreciate music and have suffered similar challenges in life may feel authentic connection through the music. Over time, the challenging experiences and feelings that motivate the artist to create music may be transformed into feelings of relief and fulfillment. The experiences of suffering that provide the original motivation to create music no longer hold power in the musician's life.

Even if the original sources of creative motivation lose power, the musician continues to experience appreciation from audiences. The authentic connection forged through the music continues to inspire others to be creative and find relief from their own sources of suffering. This feedback can inspire compassion which motivates the musician to continue sharing authentic self with others through creative expression.

Direct Creative Compassion

While inspiring authentic connection can happen through sharing creative works like art or music, for some people creativity is expressed in direct connection with others. Everyone who engages in work or activities that serve others shares direct creative connections. Teachers, clergy, health care workers, clerks and delivery people, parents and mentors are just a few examples of people who express creativity and share authentic self through direct contact with others.

As in creative product relationships, authentic direct connection relationships can bring resolution, compassion, and fulfillment to care givers, and inspiration, relief, and a sense of appreciation to care receivers.

In professional relationships like teacher-student or doctor-patient, compassion motivates the professional to receive training and to provide help and services she or he is trained to provide. In professional relationships, ethical boundaries provide guidelines as to the extent to which authentic self is shared. For example, to comfort a patient a medical professional may share his or her own similar authentic experiences. However, a medical professional would usually not share personal information as a way of establishing authentic connection.

Compassionate Presence and Boundaries

When a person experiences life threatening circumstances, direct intervention may be necessary. Direct intervention is necessary and appropriate in circumstances where food, housing, medical attention, or other life preserving assistance is needed. In life threatening circumstances, the power of compassionate presence is manifest in actions that directly provide assistance.

Outside of life-threatening circumstances, attempts to intervene directly in the lives of others can be viewed as controlling and unhelpful.

Authentic and compassionate presence cannot be forced on another person. Like a boundary, a compassionate presence can be communicated. For example, a person can say, "I can relate to your suffering. If you want to talk, I will listen."

When authentic compassion is communicated, the other person may or may not be receptive to authentic connection. Until or unless a person is receptive, simply caring is sufficient.

Like creative work, when authentic self is offered in compassionate presence, vulnerability is exposed. And like creative work, the other person has the freedom to accept, reject, or ignore a compassionate presence. And like creative work, when authentic self is rejected or ignored, ego can rise up with feelings of hurt and defensiveness and even resentment. Release of ego can allow the offer of compassionate presence to continue.

Whether openly accepted or not, communicating compassionate intentions can bring comfort. Authentic compassionate presence does not even require a person be physically present. Just communicating authentic caring through a note or gift can provide comfort without physical presence.

While professional caregivers have training in applying boundaries that help maintain focus on care for others, nonprofessional relationships rely on understanding and maintaining personal boundaries. If compassionate intentions are rejected or met with indifference, it is important to recognize and respect boundaries set by the other person. Respecting boundaries also communicates authentic compassion.

Divine Other and Compassionate Presence

In Chapter 5, some characteristics of Divine Other are discussed. Divine Other provides compassionate presence and inspiration but does not directly control anyone. To understand the role that Divine Other plays in situations where intervention is needed, as the long-time children's PBS television show host Mr. Rogers famously said, "Look to the helpers." (Rogers, 1999 6:50-7:20). Divine Other inspires compassionate intervention through "the helpers," but does not control directly.

These characteristics of Divine Other can provide a powerful lesson to persons practicing compassionate presence. Other than circumstances in which lifesaving intervention is necessary, the role of compassionate presence is to inspire rather than to control.

Authentic Relationship

Knowledge and acceptance of authentic self creates the conditions where sharing authentic self is possible. Acceptance of others allows others to share their authentic selves in kind. The goal of all this acceptance and authentic sharing is authentic relationship.

Most people are very aware of the vulnerability associated with authentic sharing, so layers of ego and identity are maintained for protection. When a person is accepted, a safe space is formed in which sharing authentic self is possible.

To glimpse the authentic self of another person is a great honor. A creative work that inspires others represents the epitome of human creative potential. Sharing a creative work that inspires another human being to pause, look inward, take a deep breath, and perhaps smile provides a great sense of fulfillment.

When creative work is direct, as is the case for people working in service to others, acceptance creates safe space for the person receiving help. In medical service, safe space allows a patient to honestly share concerns about physical ailments. In therapeutic service, acceptance and safe space allows persons to share emotional and psychological concerns. In spiritual formation and discernment, acceptance and safe space allows another person to share core beliefs based in religious and cultural origins.

In other service professions, acceptance and safe space creates an environment where a person can learn from a teacher, safely purchase a product, or enjoy a meal or a cup of coffee. Acceptance provides assurance that the service person holds no prejudice or ill will that may take advantage or cause harm to another person.

In summary, acceptance of self and other is a key part of compassion and of authentic creative work. Releasing ego-based expectations for self, others, and relationships allows authentic relationships to form. And healthy boundaries replace subconscious ego-based protections, and allow conscious choice of how and when sharing is appropriate and safe.

Exercise: Authentic Relationships and Creative Expression

Consider answering these questions as an aid in developing and sharing creative gifts:

- Are your creative gifts expressed more directly or indirectly? Through service or creative product?
- Can you think of any life challenges that motivate your creative expression?
- Have you ever experienced or provided direct intervention help? (example: Calling 911 for medical emergency)
- Have you ever experienced or provided Compassionate Presence without intervention?
- What has been your reaction to rejection or indifference to your creative efforts?
- Have you ever experienced or provided supportive and helpful critique?
- Are there any opportunities for healthy external boundaries in your life?
- Are there any opportunities for healthy internal boundaries in your life?
- Have you ever experienced or offered unconditional acceptance?

Practice:

While the previous practice focuses on developing awareness of ego-based expectations in the relationship plane, this practice focusses on authentic relationships and compassion. Acceptance of self and other is emphasized. This practice intentionally offers authentic presence to others without expecting reciprocation of any kind.

The practice again begins with a comfortable and upright posture. Diaphragm centered breathing begins, recognizing your stomach rising and falling with each breath. With every breath, distractions are recognized and released.

Breathe and visualize the consciousness plane. Inhale and exhale, releasing waking consciousness. Inhale and exhale again, releasing subconscious feelings. With another inhale and exhale, release deep instinctual feelings.

Step inside your sacred flow and breathe. Using your diaphragm, inhale and recognize consciousness energy from above flowing through your mind, your body, and your root. Exhale and recognize life energy flowing from below through your root, your body, and your mind. Visualize this flow of energy with every breath, mind to root and root to mind, inhale, and exhale.

After several breaths, move your attention into your mind chakra. Allow a cleansing inhale to sweep into your mind and allow your exhale to release confusing thoughts. Moving attention to your heart chakra, allow an inhale to bring cleansing, and an exhale to release attachments. Moving attention to your core chakra, an inhale brings cleansing, and an exhale releases fears and aversions. Finally, move attention to your root chakra. Inhale to fill your root with cleansing breath, and exhale to release obsessions.

Recognize the peaceful emptiness that comes with inner cleansing. Rest in the emptiness for a moment, breathing. Open your awareness physically and spiritually to your surrounding environment. Sounds and feelings, light and energy drift and flow through your body, as if you were transparent. With every breath, enjoy the sensation of unattached freedom.

Now from the state of emptiness, inhale and invite Divine Other to occupy your mind. With an exhale, recognize the presence of the gift of clarity. Inhale and invite Divine Love to occupy your heart. Exhale and recognize the presence of Grace. Inhale again and invite Divine Faith to fill your core. Exhale and recognize tranquility. With one more inhale, invite Divine Joy to fill your root. Exhale and smile. Relax for a moment and enjoy the sensation of Divine Other flowing from mind to root.

Now with a single breath, allow your Divine Self to rise from your root through your core, your heart, and your mind. Breathe and recognize the Communion that exists between yourself and Divine Other. Breathe and visualize your core essence radiating clarity, love, faith, and joy. Allow yourself to smile.

Now visualize your sacred essence expanding into your layers of consciousness. Breathe and expand into your neurological instinct layer. Breathe again and expand into your subconscious layer. Allow soothing and reassuring sacred core energy to accept all situational identities without judgment or expectation. Finally, breathe and expand into waking consciousness. Smile. Mindfully accept your Authentic Self. You are beautiful. You are Sacred. You are Human.

With a relaxed breath, imagine your consciousness expanding beyond the boundary of your skin.

Allow your attention to drift to an individual, perhaps an intimate partner, in this plane. Recognize this person's unique and beautiful

Sacred nature. Recognize the human challenges this person endures. Recognize the existence of this person's unique attachments and fears. Recognize the natural presence of ego-based expectations. Allow your feelings of compassion to radiate out from your heart. Be present without judgment, and without expectation. Allow your authentic, unconditional love to be present. With every breath, imagine being fully present with this person.

Moving outward, recognize your very close family and friend relationships. Recognize each of them for their own Sacred nature. Recognize each of them for their own unique humanity. Recognize the challenges they face, the attachments and fears, and the expectations they hold for themselves and others. Allow compassion to radiate from your heart to flood this layer of the relationship plane. Breathe deeply and accept.

Take a moment to rest before moving to the next layer. Remember to breathe.

Moving your consciousness outward, recognize relationships with friends and coworkers. Allow yourself to be fully present. With each breath, recognize the egos and expectations working in their lives. Some of them tend to be sources of Spiritual energy, others tend to demand Spiritual energy. Recognize, accept, and release any judgment you may harbor, and try to focus on acceptance. Recognize how they have their own attachments and fears. Everyone is Sacred. Everyone is human. Breathe, accept, and simply be present. There is no need for energy to flow from you or toward you. Being present is enough. Allow your feelings of compassion to radiate outward from your heart.

There may be an individual in this plane who draws your attention. Perhaps this person endures challenges. Perhaps this person experiences joy. Perhaps the compassion you feel yearns to help relieve this person's suffering. Recognize that your presence is a great gift whether accepted or not. Recognize that accepting this person is the greatest gift you can give. Simply breathe and be present.

Take a moment to breathe and relax.

Now expand your awareness to include acquaintances. These are people you encounter every day, people with whom you exchange polite greetings. These people include grocery store cashiers, stockers, and managers, bank tellers, and children and grandparents in parks. Even actors in movies and videos, and musicians on the radio can be included among casual acquaintances. Recognize the creative gift each of them offers. Recognize their vulnerabilities. Allow your compassion to rise.

There may be an individual you have encountered recently who draws your attention. Recognize the humanity behind the casual acquaintance. Recognize the Sacred nature of the other person. Recognize the other person's humanity. Appreciate the attachments and fears this person holds. Recognize the hopes and sacrifices this individual makes every day. Accept this person. Allow compassion and appreciation to radiate from your heart.

Now, take a moment to release all relationships to the care of each their own Higher Power. Recognize your own lack of control in the lives of others, and simply appreciate the gift of being present.

Imagine once again standing on the edge of your awareness. Gaze out at the vast expanse of humanity and life that is outside your awareness. Recognize the range of ages, genders, races, and cultures. Recognize the sacred nature of each and every living being. Recognize the suffering and mortality each one endures. Breathe and accept; accept and breathe. There is no controlling the experiences of others. Acceptance is the only option.

Appreciate the commonalities as well as the differences between yourself and others. Recognize everyone's need for authentic companionship and love.

As you gaze into the vastness, recognize that each life is individual, and that each life is sacred. Breathe and be present. Accept the attachments, the fears, the love, and the faith that each individual carries. Appreciate the potential for creative fulfillment, and the challenges of ego and subconscious identity that each living being holds. Recognize that each living being holds within a Sacred Core and the presence of Divine Other. Allow your love and compassion to radiate from your heart.

Once again, allow yourself to return to within the bounds of your own skin. Breathe and relax. Energy flows from your internal resources, from Divine Consciousness and Divine Life energy. With every breath, experience restoration.

Allow yourself to feel positive intentions toward yourself. Consider the living people and creatures near you within your home and property. Allow yourself to feel positive intentions toward them. Imagine the people and living creatures in your local neighborhood and town. Include plants, trees, fish in the streams, and animals. Breathe and extend positive intentions. Moving outward, allow yourself to feel positive intentions toward everyone in your state or province and in your country. Finally, allow your positive intentions to extend to the entire world.

With one final cleansing breath, emerge from your meditation.

11 COMMUNION OF SAINTS

In the previous chapter, the formation of authentic relationships through release of ego centered expectations is discussed. Healthy boundaries are described as an intentional way of respecting the sacred autonomy of self and others. Creativity is described as a way of sharing authentic self with others and inspiring others as well. Compassion is described as an act of being authentically present for self and others, as well as motivation for sharing creativity.

While previous chapters explored having compassion for self and others, this chapter considers accepting compassion from immanent and transcendent others in relationships. As part of this exploration, loss, grief, and the possibility of life after death are considered. Compassion is explored as a response to grief. Conscious communication, compassionate presence, and nondual energy flow in the relationship plane are discussed as well. The practice explores communion with "saints" within the relationship plane of consciousness.

Narrative:

His airway was compromised, and he was panicking. His wife had called paramedics who were on their way. He was a young man at the time, 35 years old. Although he had been exposed to the possibility of death on a few occasions, his own mortality was something he had never really considered.

Instinctive neurochemicals rushed in. His heart raced, creating more demand

144

for already limited oxygen. A metallic taste of copper filled his mouth. He began to feel light headed.

At that moment, his thoughts turned to his Christian faith. He reached up with his hands and called out for Jesus and the Apostles to be near and to be present with him. He called the Apostles out by name, Peter, John, Paul, and Mary, the mother of Jesus. And, he felt their presence. He envisioned himself with them, all standing, in a circle, hand in hand and arm in arm. He kept calling, to Francis of Assisi, James the brother of Jesus, and to his grandmother who had passed when he was a baby. He felt comforted and uplifted.

His breathing calmed; the copper taste in his mouth subsided; and he relaxed.

The paramedics arrived. He told them he did not need their services. His wife was confused, but accepting. The crisis had passed. Later he recognized this experience as a Communion of Saints.

Existential Realities and Grief

While physically alive, humans experience joy and sorrow, pleasure and pain, companionship and loneliness, and birth and death. The existential realities of living in this universe give rise to loss, suffering, and loneliness.

The physical universe is structured such that living creatures have a finite existence. Both instinct and the human capacity to recognize self-existence seem incompatible with the reality of finite existence. Finite existence results in loss of others, and eventually loss of self in death.

The human reaction to loss is suffering, in the form of grief. Just as loss is a part of existence, grieving is wired into the human condition. Grief is a natural and necessary part of being human in this universe.

Loss that triggers grief is not restricted to encountering death; any loss can trigger grief. For example, an injury or illness can result in a loss of confidence in one's health. Accidents can result in a loss of confidence in one's ability to drive or move about freely. Loss or change of a job can trigger grief, as can moving one's residence, or any number of other life changing events.

Dr. Elizabeth Kubler-Ross famously characterized grief as a process that involves five phases, including denial, anger, bargaining, depression, and acceptance (Kubler-Ross, 1969). These phases are not experienced in the same order by everyone, and multiple phases can be experienced simultaneously. Even decades after a person experiences acceptance and closure, grief can be triggered anew.

Compassion as a Response to Grief

While suffering, loss, and grief are conditions common to all human beings, compassion is also a common response to suffering, loss, and grief. When a person is grieving, compassion from others can help reduce the suffering associated with grief.

Unfortunately, grieving can also create barriers to recognizing compassion from others. When a person is in denial, recognizing compassion requires an acknowledgement that a loss has occurred. Recognizing compassion can bring a response of anger, and bargaining can result in blame directed toward a compassionate person. And, like denial, depression often wants no contact with compassionate others.

Even people skilled and practiced in mindfulness can have difficulty accepting compassion. Grief is a process that occurs at the innermost instinct layer of consciousness, where the entire focus is on protecting self from further suffering. When a person is just not ready to recognize compassion, offering a kind response of "I'm just not ready to process this yet" may be necessary.

While ideally compassion is offered in a nonjudging and noncontrolling way, in actual practice no one is perfect. People who feel compassion can become impatient with grief over time, and offer a variety of "solutions" that may or may not be helpful. Many times, when dealing with well-meaning people, a grieving person recognizes a need to be patient and compassionate in return.

While grief is processed at the instinct level of consciousness, compassion is also experienced at the instinct level. Connecting at the instinct level exposes one's existential vulnerabilities, and requires a great deal of trust.

When a person feels very alone in grief, faith in Transcendent Other can be helpful. Belief in Transcendent Other can provide a sense of comforting, noncontrolling, and nonjudging Presence. Belief in Transcendent Other can also be helpful as a person moves through the stages of grief. For example, during anger and bargaining phases of grief, anger and blame directed at Higher Power are common. Whereas family and friends might feel hurt or powerless, Transcendent Other has the capacity to abide and accept anger and blame without judgement.

Evolution and Continuing Consciousness:

One of the perhaps unavoidable questions that arises when a life is lost is whether consciousness continues in some form after death. People with faith in Transcendent Other sometimes use the belief that life continues after death to support denial of the loss. The realization eventually comes that regardless of one's beliefs, the loss is real in the physical reality of life in this universe.

To the best of our knowledge, material existence as we know it began with the Big Bang. A primordial seed was the source of everything in the universe, including galaxies, stars, planets, and eventually, life. Nondual phenomena sprang forth from the singularity, namely space-time and energy-matter.

Nondual characteristics share unique relationships, as they can be interchanged depending on point of view. For example, there is a direct relationship between time and space as expressed in distance. One could say "I sat in the airplane for five hours and traveled two thousand miles," or one could say "I traveled two thousand miles, and it took five hours to do so." Either way, the same meaning is conveyed with time and distance being interchangeable terms.

Modern physics has demonstrated a similar relationship between energy and matter. When matter is destroyed, a great deal of energy is released according to the relationship defined by Einstein's famous equation, $e=mc^2$. Matter and energy have a shared and interchangeable relationship just as space-time have a shared and interchangeable relationship.

Energy-Matter and Space-Time also interact with each other. Gravity, the weight a person feels and measures with a scale, is experienced as an acceleration that results from space-time being curved by the mass of an object. A very large accumulation of mass can curve space-time to the extent that stars or even black holes are formed.

There is a property of space-time-energy-matter that is particularly interesting. The second law of thermodynamics predicts that over time, all systems break down and dissipate until they reach a stable rest state. For example, some stars, like camp fires, eventually use up their fuel and burn out. (Depending on their mass, other stars may explode or collapse into black holes, but the same law applies.) The release of energy until a stable state is reached is known as entropy.

As stars use up energy and increase entropy, new stable elements are formed. Eventually, this process of using up energy within stars forms elements like carbon and oxygen which are the building blocks for sustaining physical life.

Characteristics of living creatures described in previous chapters include breath (Ruach in Hebrew), and consciousness (Nephesh in Hebrew). The Ruach / Nephesh characteristics of life also share a nondual relationship. Life gives rise to consciousness, and consciousness expands and responds to the needs for sustaining life.

Unlike energy-matter-space-time, life does not obey the laws of increasing entropy, in fact quite the opposite. With evolution, life becomes more complicated and accumulates more energy. DNA strands grow longer, and consciousness gains more capacity for intelligence. Rather than reducing in complication, evolving life increases in complication over time, and entropy is decreased. To repeat this for emphasis, space-time-energy-mass which breaks down over time, interacting with Ruach-Nephesh-Spirit, produces life-consciousness that evolves into more complex forms.

While life gets more complex through the process of evolution, growth of consciousness also develops during the span of any single lifetime. After a living creature reaches maturity, life continues and consciousness continues to grow in knowledge and experience. Eventually, life ends. Matter without Spirit resumes the course of increasing entropy, breaking down into constituent stable elements.

Continuing Consciousness

The first law of thermodynamics states that in any closed system the total amount of mass-energy is preserved over time. While energy may dissipate and matter may take a stable state, the total amount of energy and matter remains constant. Energy that dissipates remains in existence. When the conservation principle is applied to Spirit, the possibility is revealed that life-consciousness energy remains in existence even after physical life ends.

People in some cultures believe in consciousness being preserved through reincarnation; others believe in ultimate healing and reconciliation in incorruptible physical bodies. Some people believe consciousness joins or rejoins a Divine Other. Other people believe in a developing collective consciousness that is part of the structure of the universe.

In her book "On Life after Death" (Kubler-Ross, 1991), Elizabeth

Kubler Ross describes three stages of experience that many dying people share regardless of age or culture. The first stage she describes is the physical body reaching a point where it can no longer sustain life.

The second stage is experiencing freedom from the physical body, and existence in a restored state. Lost limbs appear to be present, sight is restored to blind people, and any sensations of pain are gone. She shares many cases in which people who have been resuscitated from death describe in detail the room in which their physical body lies, and the people working to restore their physical life.

The third stage has two components. Trusted and beloved family members, friends, or saints associated with one's culture are often said to appear. And this is true regardless of culture, whether Christian, Jewish, Muslim, Buddhist, or other. Trusted saints are present to accompany a person into a warm, inviting source of light. Moving toward the light is said to feel like returning to one's home.

It is possible that the singularity-seed that formed the universe was set in place by Divine Other Consciousness. It is possible that the universe itself is an emerging collective consciousness, ever growing in compassion, love, awareness, and knowledge until the origins are understood and true full communion with the Divine Other Consciousness is achieved.

Whatever the source and whatever spiritual mechanics guide the development of life and consciousness, there is hope. The fact that human consciousness includes the characteristic of hopefulness is in itself hopeful. There is hope for continuing consciousness and ultimate healing and reconciliation that resolves the existential experiences of suffering, death, and separation.

Consciousness Communication

Even after death, consciousness carries on in the physical universe through shared creative works. Creative works provide a medium through which relationships can form between the creative person and an audience. Creative works provide symbols that convey meaning. Languages are composed of symbols that convey meaning. Both music and words are conveyed through composition language. Creative media, like paintings, pictures, movies, and videos also provide symbols that convey meaning.

Some symbols take on meaning that transcend words. Religious symbols, like the Christian Cross, the Taoist Yin Yang, and Om symbol from Hinduism and Buddhism contain meanings that resonate and are shared through history and cultures.

What happens when a person encounters a symbol? If the symbol has meaning for a person, the symbol inspires memories and emotions. If the symbol is a source of deep spiritual meaning, a resonance occurs through the consciousness layers and harmonizes with the Sacred Core.

In this LLCA consciousness model, Sacred Core in communion with Divine Other resonates with instinct level neurochemicals and all layers of consciousness. Sacred Core continues to resonate and connect outside the physical body through connections made in the relationship plane.

With acceptance of self and other and the release of ego-based expectations, relationships approach genuine person to person connection. Whether connecting through creative symbols or direct interaction, authentic relationship, resonating with spiritual energy, can feel like a direct consciousness to consciousness connection, transcending physical boundaries.

The question of whether direct consciousness to consciousness contact without the benefit of shared symbols or direct physical contact is possible has been considered and explored since the earliest times of human existence. Anecdotal witness to direct communication with transcended and transcendent beings represents a major part of religious tradition and culture. Stories of contact with angels and demons, gins, dakas, and dakinis, saints, muses and ghosts are shared in every human culture.

Some witnesses describe not only consciousness to consciousness communication, but also direct conscious manipulation of matter, in the form of seemingly miraculous events and interventions. Some traditions describe conscious or spiritual energy resonating through physical objects, crystals, and even spirit animals.

Is direct consciousness contact without the benefit of symbols, language, or physical contact possible? Massive accumulated anecdotal witness from across human history and experience suggests that yes, direct consciousness interaction is possible. Science, however, has yet to provide direct, repeatable evidence that consciousness interactions are possible when controls are used during observation.

Experiencing Compassionate Presence

Conscious resonance, whether invoked through relationships, symbols, or direct consciousness to consciousness contact, absolutely does manifest inspiration. Neurochemical, emotional, subconscious, and conscious feelings, thoughts, and actions can be influenced through inspiration. Regardless of the source, the effects of inspiration are real.

Sharing creative works inspires creativity in others, and compassionate presence eases suffering, reconciles relationships, and creates conditions that encourage healing. Relationships provide an opportunity to share experiences. When common experiences are shared, mutual compassion and love are cultivated. The experience of shared love and compassion helps to soften the existential realities of mortality and singular existence. Indeed, sharing creative gifts and mutual love helps to prolong life and bring hope and meaning to existence.

Experiencing companionship and love produces the neurochemical oxytocin in the instinct layer of consciousness. Gentle touching, close companionship, and even petting a dog or cat can release oxytocin into the nervous system (Uvnäs-Moberg, Handlin & Petersson, 2015). As oxytocin flows, resonant spiritual love energy flows from the heart chakra. A resonance of companionship in relationship is established.

Nondual Energy Flow

A person who recognizes and releases sources of suffering and engages in creativity to the benefit of self and others lives a nondual existence enjoying life, love, and freedom, while also recognizing limitations such as suffering and death. The principles and practices of releasing attachments and aversions allows a person freedom to experience faith and love and joy, and to develop and share creativity. The mortal suffering that remains with the self and others serves as motivation for continued compassion expressed through creative engagement.

Nonduality recognizes the "both-and" nature of existence, which includes suffering and joy, loss and companionship, and individuality and connection with others. Nonduality recognizes that that while the existential realities of mortality exist, the saintly community of compassionate beings also exists. Nonduality recognizes that we are alone, and we are not alone. We are singular beings isolated from others within each our own flesh-based existence, and we are part of the vast communal relationship plane.

When considering the vast relationship plane that encompasses all of space-time, one might visualize saintly sources of compassion as sources of light within the plane. Like gazing up at the night sky, millions and billions of sources of compassionate energy may be recognized. These points of light are sources of positive spiritual energy.

The relationship plane also includes points of darkness where spiritual energy is absorbed. When engaged, these points of dark consciousness can also resonate with a person's sacred core, and in the process drain spiritual energy. Negative inspiration that comes from spiritual draining consciousness can result in fear, attachments, and confusion. Negative inspiration can spread to others, creating a web of suffering and spiritual energy drain.

While most conscious beings carry both light and dark energy, dark consciousnesses tends to be isolated from internal Divine Other Spiritual Energy sources of life and consciousness, Ruach and Nephesh. Without access to Divine Other internally, dark consciousness draws and drains spiritual energy from external sources. While saintly beings hold great compassion for those who suffer, saintly beings also recognize the necessity for healthy boundaries and protection of self. In the practice of Communion of Saints, sources of light are recognized and accepted with gratitude.

Communion of Saints

For every conscious being who reaches out to others with compassion, there are millions of others who do likewise in return. Conscious beings who reach out in compassion may be living or may have moved past physical existence. Like beacons of light in the relationship plane, compassionate conscious beings are everywhere and from every time; past, present, and future.

Communion of Saints acknowledges the presence of compassionate others, both living and passed on. Communion of Saints acknowledges a community of conscious beings who have the capacity for and the will to share love and compassion with all other living creatures. Everyone who reaches out in compassion, including LLCA participants, are part of this community of compassionate beings.

In the Divine Communion practice of Chapter 5, the presence of Divine Other is invited into the Sacred Core to inspire creativity, love, faith, and joy. In Communion of Saints, love centered conscious beings throughout space and time are acknowledged and accepted. As is the case with physical companionship, Communion of Saints can inspire oxytocin flow, which creates resonant love energy within the Sacred Core. An unparalleled sense of companionship and belonging can be experienced when a communion of saints is experienced.

Nearly all cultures and religions carry rich histories and traditions of saints, scholars, and loving and beloved conscious beings.

In the Mahayanist Buddhist tradition, Bodhisattvas are saintly beings who have experienced liberation from suffering and choose to remain a conscious presence and resource for all living creatures. (Padmakara Translation Group, 1997)

In Christianity, revered saintly beings include Francis of Assisi, the Apostles Peter, John, and Paul, and Mary the mother of Jesus, as well as many others.

Prophets, Saints, and scholars are also revered within Judaism and Islam. Buddhist and Hindu traditions also revere saints and scholars. Native and Indigenous shamans revere the memories of healers and saintly ancestors and guides. In Japanese and other cultures, family members living and passed on are remembered and revered.

When considering family and friends who have passed on, the human challenges and mistakes that result in suffering of self and others are often remembered as well. Many traditions also carry hope for ultimate healing and reconciliation for those who have passed on. Belief in ultimate healing and reconciliation can bring comfort in loss, and can bring forgiveness and reconciliation to difficult relationships. Communion of Saints can include relationships that were less than perfect during physical life.

While LLCA recognizes communion between Divine Other and Sacred Core, nontheistic and atheistic beings are not excluded as sources of compassionate presence. As in all things, a tree is known by the fruit it bears. Where there is kindness, love, peace, and compassion, there is Divine Spirit.

Exercise: Discerning Community of Saints

- How does your religion / culture of origin view Continuation of Consciousness after death?
  - Which model of continuing consciousness appeals to you?
    - Reincarnation and ongoing Conscious Development
    - Ultimate healing and Reconciliation
    - Join / rejoin Divine Other Consciousness
    - Join developing Collective Consciousness
    - Ending of life, consciousness, and suffering
    - Other - Describe
- Have you ever experienced "Consciousness to consciousness" communication, with living or passed on Beings? Describe?
  - Do any cultural or religious symbols resonate deeply with you?
- Of the Beings you have known and are aware of, living and passed on, who would you consider as part of your "Community of Saints"?

Practice:

While previous practices focus on accepting and sharing internal sources of restorative spiritual energy, this practice focuses on recognizing and accepting the restorative compassionate presence of others.

Begin the practice by sitting in a comfortable and upright position and breathing with your diaphragm. With each cleansing breath, recognize your stomach rising and falling. Breathe. Recognize, accept, and release any external noise distractions. Breathe. Recognize, accept, and release any physical distractions. Breathe again and recognize, accept, and release any distracting thoughts and feelings.

Inhale and imagine yourself releasing consciousness layers, moving your attention inward. Exhale and release waking consciousness. Release subconscious ego. Release instinctual protective egos.

Inhale again and imagine cleansing your sacred core energy centers. Exhale and release distracting thoughts from your mind. Release attachments and resentments from your heart. Release fears and aversions from your core. Release obsessions from your root.

Rest in this state of emptiness for a moment. Focus on your breathing. Allow yourself to experience nonattached freedom, as if light and sounds pass right through you. Allow yourself to recognize spiritual energies that ebb and flow throughout the universe.

With a small, silent prayer, invite Divine Other to expand into your chakra energy centers. With a single breath, accept clarity, love, faith, and joy. Imagine Divine Energy flowing within your Sacred Core.

With another breath, recognize your Divine self, rising in communion with Divine Other. Recognize the rising of joy, faith, love, and clarity within your Sacred Core. Recognize Divine Ruach life flowing in sacred communion with Divine Nephesh consciousness.

Now breathe again and allow your sacred core consciousness to radiate outward, fulfilling your consciousness layers. Instinct, subconscious, and consciousness layers are cleansed. Clarity, love, peace, and joy resonate throughout your layers of consciousness.

Take a moment again to breathe. Allow peace and joy to permeate your being. Focus on the movement of your diaphragm. Just breathe.

Now, allow your attention to reach outside of your consciousness into the relationship plane. Recognize the points of light that surround you. Some are close at hand in beloved family members. Some are farther away, representing beloved mentors and teachers. Every point of light contains compassionate presence. Recognize that these bright lights represent both living beings and beloved saints who have passed on and whose consciousness continues to shine with love and compassion.

With gratitude, take a moment to accept the compassionate light from these saintly beings. Allow compassion from others to resonate with your own consciousness. Recognize the flow of oxytocin that comes with accepting compassionate presence.

Looking further, recognize the compassionate light that represents artists from within your own culture. Music, images, and symbols flow with light and love. Breathe deeply and allow the music and symbols to resonate with your core consciousness. Breathe and experience the compassionate communion with luminous beings whose consciousness continues to shine and resonate.

Recognize the light of compassion that flows from saintly beings. Names like Mary, Francis, and Desmond Tutu may come to mind. Names like Thich Nhat Hahn, and Gandhi may also come to mind. Other revered saints and scholars from your own culture may also be recognized. With every breath, recognize these sources of light, dedicated to sharing compassion and love with the universe.

As oxytocin flows, you may experience emotions of joy and

comfort. Accept these feelings with gratitude. Continue to breathe. With every inhale, accept the communion experience. With every exhale, allow your own light to shine and resonate. Recognize that you also are a source of light in this consciousness plane. You are a star that glows among the vast universe of stars. You are a song that resonates in the vast chorus of singers. Breathe. Breathe again. Breathe again. Continue to breathe and experience this exchange of light energy for several minutes.

With a sense of gratitude, return your attention to your own conscious being. Allow positive intentions, toward yourself and toward others near you within your household and among your neighbors. Allow positive intentions toward animals on the ground, fish in streams, and birds in the air. Extend your positive intentions to include your local town, parish and county, state, and province. Allow your positive intentions to extend to everyone within your nation and country and toward everyone and everything in the entire world.

With gratitude, with love and compassion, and with intentional breathing, open your eyes. Recognize that although the practice has ended, your light and the light of others remains. Always abiding, always present, always faithful, hopeful, and always loving.

12 NONDUAL FULFILLMENT

In the previous chapter, the evolution of consciousness, and the possibility of consciousness persisting after physical death are explored. Loss, grief, and the possibility of life after death are discussed. Compassion as a response to grief is explored. Conscious communication is explored in the context of experiencing compassionate presence. Spiritual energy flow and accepting love and compassion in "Communion of Saints" are also discussed.

Early in this program, models for consciousness layers and spiritual energy centers (or chakras) are introduced. Models are used to help understand how human beings think, feel, and interact. The models are holistic in that they describe spiritual, physical/neurochemical, emotional, and relationship influences.

Early meditative practices explore breath centered stabilization and release of attachments and energy blockages that cause suffering and pain.

Divine Other is described as the source of Consciousness/ Nephesh energy, and life / Ruach energy. Sacred Core self is introduced as a center for life and consciousness that is creative and unique and exists in communion with Divine Other. The concepts of compassion and forgiveness are introduced in the context of developing compassion for self. Protective and situational identities are introduced as subconscious ego-selves, and compassion is cultivated for ego-selves as well.

The model for consciousness is expanded beyond physical boundaries to include personal, casual, and undeveloped relationships. The role that ego plays in setting expectations for self, others, and relationships is explored. Authentic presence is described in terms of compassion for others and sharing one's authentic self through healthy relationships and creative expression. Sharing authentic presence is also described in terms of communion with authentic others and recognizing both immanent and transcendent compassionate loving presence.

In this chapter, deeper concepts of meaning and purpose are explored as motivation for cultivating and sharing creative gifts. The roles of existential challenges in forming meaning and purpose are discussed from long term evolutionary and Spiritual perspectives, and from a single lifespan perspective. Cultivating and sharing creativity are explored as a means for mitigating suffering and nurturing healing and reconciling love. In the practice, the concept of authentic relationship is expanded to include the sharing of Sacred Core Divine Energy in "Namaste" relationship.

Narrative

She rose from her meditation feeling grateful, loved, secure, and curious. She reflected upon how her own personal development had progressed over her lifetime. She had discovered and developed her gifts to the extent that they not only benefited others, but they provided sustenance as well. Letting go of the expectations she held for herself, others, and relationships had allowed her to connect authentically and experience real love. While life's losses and tragedies continued to generate feelings of sorrow and grief, she recognized that all suffering and losses had meaning and purpose. Her experiences and challenges helped her to develop patience, tolerance, and compassion, which she recognized as characteristics of wisdom. She was able to simply be present for others and maintain boundaries for her own well-being. She saw the cycles of life, suffering, death, and joy from a larger context, as part of a universe that was ever increasing in creative self-awareness, compassion, and love. She believed that a Guiding Light worked within creation and all living things, illuminating a path toward a greater purpose. When suffering brought by ignorance and cruelty threatened her peace, her faith brought comfort. She truly believed that all things worked together to increase nondual awareness, reconciliation, and love. She was grateful for her own existence and participation in the Great Communion of Saints, Life, and Consciousness.

Creative Evolution

All the concepts and models from previous chapters are discussed with one major thesis in mind: developing and sharing creative gifts for the benefit of self and others. The foundation that supports the thesis throughout is compassion and love that transcends existential limitations of mortality and singular existence.

In previous chapters evolution of life is described, from the earliest single celled creatures dependent on volcanic vents, to autonomous and sacred human beings. The response of consciousness to existential challenges was initially pure instinct. The simple instructions seeking nourishment and comfort while avoiding discomfort and death were direct responses to the existential realities of suffering and loss. The drive to procreate provided a direct response to the existential reality of singular existence.

One only needs to observe a reptile abandoning offspring in eggs to fend for themselves in contrast to humans raising children for decades to recognize an evolutionary trend toward compassion and nurture. Human willingness to sacrifice self in service to family and community proves the point further. Pure instinct directed toward survival and comfort for self takes a back seat to caring for the well-being of others. For many, compassion extends beyond the limits of community and even humanity to include all living creatures and even creation itself. Humanity, it seems, reveals the universe's purpose in increasing love, community, and self-awareness. Conscious creative development and sharing is the means through which the universe becomes self-aware.

Human creativity is motivated by both survival instinct and compassion to address existential challenges, mitigate suffering, and nurture healing and communal well-being. Human creativity drives us to learn about ourselves and the universe in which we live.

At the time of this writing, physicists and astronomers have invented tools like the CERN accelerator and the James Webb telescope to see deeper and further into the origins of physical existence. Biologists have mapped and adapted research toward understanding the origins of life. The quest for knowledge is driven by a desire to understand the physical and biological challenges that affect life and existence.

Cultural Perspectives on Meaning and Purpose

Nearly every tradition and culture in human history has offered perspective on the meaning and purpose of life and existence.

159

In Judaism, the purpose and meaning of life can be described as service to God in a way that benefits self, community, and others. (Tanakh, 1985 Lev 19:18). Buddhism suggests that the purpose of life is to relieve suffering through living a good and meaningful life that serves self and others. (Harvey, 1990) Christianity describes the purpose of life in terms of demonstrating love of God through care for self and service to others. (NRSV, 1989, Matt 22:36-40) Islamic theology is also centered in learning about and sharing the compassion that God expresses toward humanity with others. (The Noble Qur'an, An-Nisa 4:36)

In Hinduism, the Holy Bhagavad Ghita suggests that the purpose of existence is to release ego and perform one's duties in life. (The Bhagavad Gita, 2022) While the context of the lesson (delivering justice in battle) can be challenging for some, the underlying message is worth considering.

From all cultural perspectives, human beings have a duty and responsibility to serve in a way that benefits self and others, bringing healing and increasing communal well-being. Most cultures have specific words to describe these goals. Hindi uses the word Dharma, Hebrew Chesed, Arabic Ar Rahim, and the word used in English is Grace. Each word is used to describe unconditional love that brings healing, communion, and justice.

Meaning in Suffering

Evolution reveals a long-term trend, from instinct for survival of self toward compassion for offspring; compassion that expands to include all life and creation. Cultural records reveal a common purpose of compassionate service for the benefit of self and others.

While purpose and meaning can be discerned from the workings of nature and culture, life experiences that include births and losses, companionship and loneliness, and joy and suffering, can lead a person to question purpose and meaning on a personal level.

Given the challenges that are part of existence, a person might conclude that the universe is built on destruction and suffering. Stars are destroyed to create heavier elements that support life. Life ends in death, and the compost of death creates fertile ground for new life to flourish. The journey from birth to death is filled with suffering and loss.

Just as destruction is part of the universe, suffering is a part of physical existence. Whether the path is long and arduous or short and tragic, suffering is part of the journey. If someone dies unexpectedly and suddenly, the burden of suffering is conveyed through shock and grief to loved ones. If someone suffers over an extended time, as is the case with chronic diseases like cancer and Alzheimer's disease, the end of suffering can be experienced with some sense of relief. Either way, suffering is part of the experience.

To help discern a sense of meaning in suffering, consider the pain experienced by a woman while giving birth. Suffering experienced during the rigors of childbirth certainly has a purpose in bringing new conscious life to the universe.

Suffering also motivates compassion for self and others. When the burden of suffering is shared in compassionate presence, comfort is conveyed, the burden is lightened, and pathways to healing and reconciliation are opened.

In his book "Man's Search for Meaning," Viktor Frankl (Frankl, 1946) describes the horrors of living the enslaved deprivation of concentration camps. After describing his personal ordeal as a prisoner, he concludes that the purpose of life can be found in three ways: performing duty, loving others, and discerning meaning while experiencing suffering.

The sacred nature of life and the sacred worthiness of every living being provides motivation for preserving life and reducing suffering. Every living creature has a duty to live, love, and apply creative gifts to bring joy and reduce suffering of self and others.

Suffering met with a sense of duty can provide inspiration for others. In a previous chapter an example is mentioned where a blues musician shares the experience of suffering through his creative gift. Just as suffering can be met with a sense of duty, the sharing of experience through creative gifts is a duty that not only mitigates suffering, but also brings joy to performer and audience alike.

In his book, Frankl described how loving his wife gave him strength to carry on under terrible conditions. Even knowing that she was no longer physically alive, his ongoing relationship with her memory gave him strength.

Simply enduring suffering has meaning. Being present for self and others while enduring suffering has meaning. Determination to endure and be fully present creates opportunities for healing and reconciliation, even and especially when the suffering ends in loss or death. History is full of stories about heroes and humble individuals facing suffering and death with bravery and grace. These are the stories and experiences that bring both tears and resolve that translate to meaning and purpose.

The gift of inspiring others through enduring and compassionate presence and sharing creativity extends long past any individual's physical life time. Creative presence, compassion, and love continue in creative works and communion of saints, providing inspiration for generations to come.

Creative Development

A great deal of this program is dedicated to removing blocks to creativity and establishing motivation. Establishing sacred self-worth and the sacred worth of all living creatures provides a foundation for compassion that transcends survival instincts. Compassion for self and others provides a lifetime of motivation for developing and sharing creative gifts, for the purpose of mitigating suffering and cultivating reconciliation and healing. Once motivation is established, the emphasis shifts to developing and sharing creative gifts; in other words, doing the work of exercising creativity.

Creative gifts can be associated with chakra energy centers. Mind oriented gifts include learning, problem solving, and organizing. Heart oriented gifts include helping and healing relationships which can include medicine, ministry, teaching, and even sales. Core oriented gifts can be hands-on and can include gardening, repairing things, and even artistic physical activities like dance, yoga, cooking, physical development, and coaching. Root oriented gifts can include artistic pursuits like music, sculpture, painting, photography, movie, and video development.

Once creative gifts are determined, development is needed for reaching a level of skill in which creative gifts are productive. Development may mean engaging in schooling and connecting with mentors for training.

While skill development is worthwhile, so is flexibility. Developing a particular skillset may open doors to places a person never imagined. For example, someone who has a goal of becoming a doctor may find that being a physical therapist or pharmacist is more satisfying. Someone who is repairing cars may find more satisfaction in marketing or sales, and verse visa, someone who begins a career in sales might find that performing hands-on repairs is more satisfying. At any time while developing skills, one might find that teaching and mentoring is a more satisfying way to engage in the creative process. The point is that while goals are important, flexibility is important as well. Many doors open along any path, and some may lead to greater joy and productivity than the current path provides.

Once creative gifts are developed to a certain level, creative efforts become productive. Creative gifts can produce an endless range of useful results, including tangible art, healing and teaching relationships, garden produce and food preparation, building and repair of useful items, and many others.

Sharing Creative Gifts

Once creative gifts are developed to the point of productivity, focus shifts from exclusively learning and development to sharing. One of the necessary skills needed for sharing is marketing one's gifts. This means making connections with people who are receptive to or have need for creative products.

It may feel unnatural to shift focus from a motivation of bringing healing and reconciliation to marketing. Indeed, for persons focused on "doing the tasks," the word "marketing" can bring reactions from eye-rolling skepticism to instinctual fight or flight feelings. But how else is one to bring one's skills to the attention of persons who may benefit? How else is one to gain the personal benefits of sharing and even earning a living from one's skills?

In employment, the job usually provides infrastructure and support needed for bringing creative skills to market to be shared with people who can benefit. Even when a person is employed, self-marketing skills are required to find suitable opportunities for sharing one's creative gifts. If a person is self-employed, even greater marketing skills and resources are necessary for making creative product available to a larger audience.

Marketing one's skills also means having the strength and resilience to risk rejection. Sharing one's creative content and experience can create a sense of vulnerability. In any relationship, sharing requires some level of risk taking. Sharing invites feedback which can help refine a person's creative skills.

For many people, after a certain level of skill and experience is attained, focus moves from direct development of product and connection with others toward mentoring others who are developing similar skills. In this way, one's skills are passed on to future generations.

To summarize, the process of developing and sharing creative gifts begins with motivation and discovery of creative gifts, followed by training and development, producing useful results, and sharing those results with others. Eventually, mentoring others to develop creative skills can become a priority.

Creative Engagement and Self Care

Everyone experiences times where motivation seems low and even the most creative, joyful occupations feel unfulfilling. At these times, a sense of duty can become a prime motivator. Duty can be found in relationships with family and friends, clients, and customers, as well as toward Divine Other. Participation in the process of the universe, which always progresses toward greater love, community, and creative consciousness can provide a sense of duty as well.

While creative development and sharing can bring joy and fulfillment, mortal existence comes with its own set of demands. Every human being requires self-care. While goal-oriented people are often successful, ignoring or sacrificing physical, mental, and spiritual health in the pursuit of success limits the amount of sharing a person can engage in. Creativity itself requires a variety of supporting activities and relationships to remain fresh and alive. Healthy relationships, a joyful living environment, and healthy diet and exercise can contribute to overall joy and productivity. Engagement in hobbies outside of one's main creative focus can help bring fresh ideas that enhance overall creativity.

Along with mortal existence, being human also means being a singular entity. As such, choices often need to be made and priorities set. Internal ego selves compete for attention, including the good spouse, the good worker, the good parent, and the healthy individual. When conflicts arise, Sacred Core is available to help determine the best course moving forward.

Self-care is always a primary priority; creative engagement and sharing is restricted if a person is not healthy, emotionally happy, and spiritually connected. Fortunately, creative development and sharing also support the goals of physical, emotional, and spiritual health. The joy that comes from accomplishment and sharing creative product is uplifting. Physical activities and periods of rest while engaging in healthy relationships support the cultivation of inspiration, from others and from within, and from Divine Other. Practices like yoga, tai chi, walking, jogging, biking, and working out all support both self-care and creative development.

When self-care practices feel boring and repetitive, a change of scenery may be required. When relationships become draining, boundaries may be necessary. Sometimes healing and rest are required. While everyone occasionally feels drained and even overwhelmed, an overall organic existence in which all experiences contribute to health, joy, and creativity is possible. Consider, for example, the way the human body functions. The heart pumps; the lungs breathe; and the digestive system functions. All are mutually supportive and operate without specific attention required on any specific function. Organic living that includes self-care, creative sharing, and healthy relationships can function similarly, with all aspects mutually supportive and not competing for attention.

Maintaining Healthy Connections

While motivation, creative product, sharing, and self-care are important, so too is staying connected with peers and other supportive beings. In the last chapter connecting with and accepting compassion from others is discussed at length, including connection with saintly beings. In previous chapters connecting with Divine Other is discussed as well.

Divine Other may be understood as an idealized representation of pure light, love, clarity, faith, wisdom, and joy. Divine Other is the Source for all energies produced within Sacred Core chakras.

Sacred Core self exists in nondual Communion with Divine Other. Sacred Core self is unique and has unique gifts to offer and to share. Sacred Core self is also intimately connected with and part of Divine Other. The source of pure positive creative energy is a part of who we are as living creatures.

In previous chapters, the concept of ego is also discussed. Ego may be understood as idealized versions of self and others that get imposed into relationships. Ego can interfere with authentic connections between self and others.

Ego also represents an "automatic defense" mechanism for protecting self. As needs arise, situational identities rise-up as extensions of ego. While the goal of ego defense is to protect the individual, sometimes ego defenses can be a source of significant suffering. Mindfulness is introduced to recognize automatic ego defenses and intentionally choose responses that reduce suffering and increase joy.

If a person were able to stand outside of her or his self and look inward, that person might discern the Sacred Core shining through with creative energy. That same person might also observe clouds or shadows drifting across Sacred Core self, obscuring the light. The clouds that obscure Sacred Core self from shining outward may be understood as ego self. As the consciousness model suggests, ego self covers Sacred Core self with the intent of protection.

In extreme cases, ego may completely block Sacred Core self from shining through. If an outsider can see any light, it may be light reflected from the outsider. In this way, a Sacred Core that is completely obscured may appear attractive to others who see their own reflections. Gazing upon a purely reflective ego and seeing self has the effect of boosting one's own ego, just as the mythological character Narcissus gazed at his own beauty in a reflecting pool.

The clouds of ego do not only obscure Sacred Core light from shining outward; they also prevent Sacred Core light being received from others. When a pure ego soul looks out upon the relationship plane and sees only reflections of self, the sacred autonomy and creative beauty of others is completely obscured.

These are lonely souls who can only discern themselves.

Everyone has egos. No one shares Sacred Core self completely and perfectly. While Sacred Core self draws strength from communion with Divine Other, egos can be fragile. When the possibility of hurt or rejection is perceived, ego rushes in to shadow and protect the self. The shadowing of self is a two-edged sword; while the risk of rejection is mitigated, the ability to share love and creative energy is masked as well.

Discerning whether relationships share authentic Sacred Core energy or reflected ego energy can be difficult. The greatest indicator of authentic Sacred Core energy is compassion for others. While ego represents pure protection of self, Sacred Core energy represents pure love and light that cares about the well-being of both self and others. The degree to which a person cares for others provides a gauge of the degree to which ego shadows the Sacred Core.

Conscious beings have developed the capacity for love of self and others. The relationship plane that encompasses "love for other" is ever growing. At the most basic level, love for others includes self, family, and close friends. As the capacity for love expands, love for others grows to include all of creation.

Expanding Capacity for Love

When Sacred Core is not masked by ego, love for others can grow to include people of different races, ethnicities, and cultures. Love for others can expand to include the planet, the environment, and all living creatures.

As the capacity for love grows, so does awareness of the capacity for harm that the universe and society carries. Nearly every human heritage includes histories of oppression, exploitation, conquest, and even slavery. Indeed, most people originate from cultures that have engaged in or suffered from exploitation, oppression, and conquest of neighboring tribes and nations. Recognition of the universe's capacity for causing suffering also brings recognition that "all others" include real and perceived "enemies" who intentionally cause suffering. At times it seems the path toward "compassion for all" conflicts with protecting self and loved ones.

Of course, exposure to others who would bring harm and suffering requires healthy boundaries. But the call to love inclusively and unconditionally persists, especially in the context of sharing creative gifts that may bring healing to troubled souls.

One might ask, how can a person "love enemies" while maintaining healthy boundaries? The answer is, of course, compassion without attachment. It is possible to mindfully understand the instincts, fears, and obsessions that drive "enemies." With understanding comes compassion, accompanied by the knowledge that any desire to control, "fix," or somehow manage other living creatures simply does not work. Love abides, but does not control. Sometimes, compassion and love require protective boundaries, but like love, hope abides, seeking reconciliation and healing for all. Faith abides as well, believing that reconciliation and healing are always possible.

A lone wolf predator that only has the capacity to care for self can grow into the role of family and tribal protector. Likewise, the capacity to care for and protect family and tribe can grow into loving others outside of tribal boundaries. The nondual capacity to love self and all others, even "enemies," represents the vector along which life and consciousness are developing.

Divine Other represents the source and the fulfillment of universal development. Made in the image of Divine Other, Divine DNA guides the development of life and consciousness along the vector of ever-increasing inclusive love.

While unconditional love of Self and Other represents human potential, the reality is that individuals exist throughout the developmental spectrum, from completely lacking the capacity to love others, to the full capacity to love all others unconditionally.

Exercise: Cultivating and Sharing Creativity

This is a brainstorming exercise, where first thoughts that come to mind are written down. This exercise explores how the various chapters and practices in this program have contributed to your cultivating and sharing of creative gifts.

1. Prior to entering this program, what were your major blockages to developing and sharing love and creativity? Please frame your answers in relation to chakra energies – confusion, attachments, aversions, and obsessions.

2. Can you identify situational and protection ego identities that have been especially challenging to developing and sharing love and creativity? Can you identify ego identities that have been encouraging?

3. Have the practices been helpful in developing and sharing love and creativity? How so?

4. Has your understanding of and relationship with Divine Other evolved through this program? How so?

5. Has compassion for yourself evolved through this program? Has your compassion for others evolved?

6. Which creative gifts do you feel have been encouraged for development and sharing? Are your gifts more physically artistic, or relational and helping? How are your gifts both physical and relational?

7. Have your relationships changed through this program? Can you describe examples where boundaries have been improved? Can you describe examples where you risked vulnerability?

8. How would you describe your motivation for creative development and sharing? How has your motivation changed since beginning this program?

9. How are you sharing your creative gifts personally? Professionally?

10. How has your ability to handle life's challenges evolved through this program?

11. Has your ability to accept compassion and help from others evolved through this program? Do any examples come to mind?

12. Has your capacity for sharing love and compassion evolved? How so?

Divine Namaste

In the previous chapter, acceptance of compassionate love energy in a "Communion of Saints" is discussed. Love energy from others radiates through the relationship plane, permeates through waking conscious, ego subconscious, and instinct protection layers, and resonates with Sacred Core.

In prior chapters, compassionate love energy from within is described in a similar manner. Love energy originating from within the Sacred Core resonates with and permeates through neurochemical instincts, subconscious egos, and waking consciousness to be shared with others.

In both giving and receiving, love energy originates in communion with Divine Other. The exchange of love energy in compassionate relationship is represented in the following diagram:

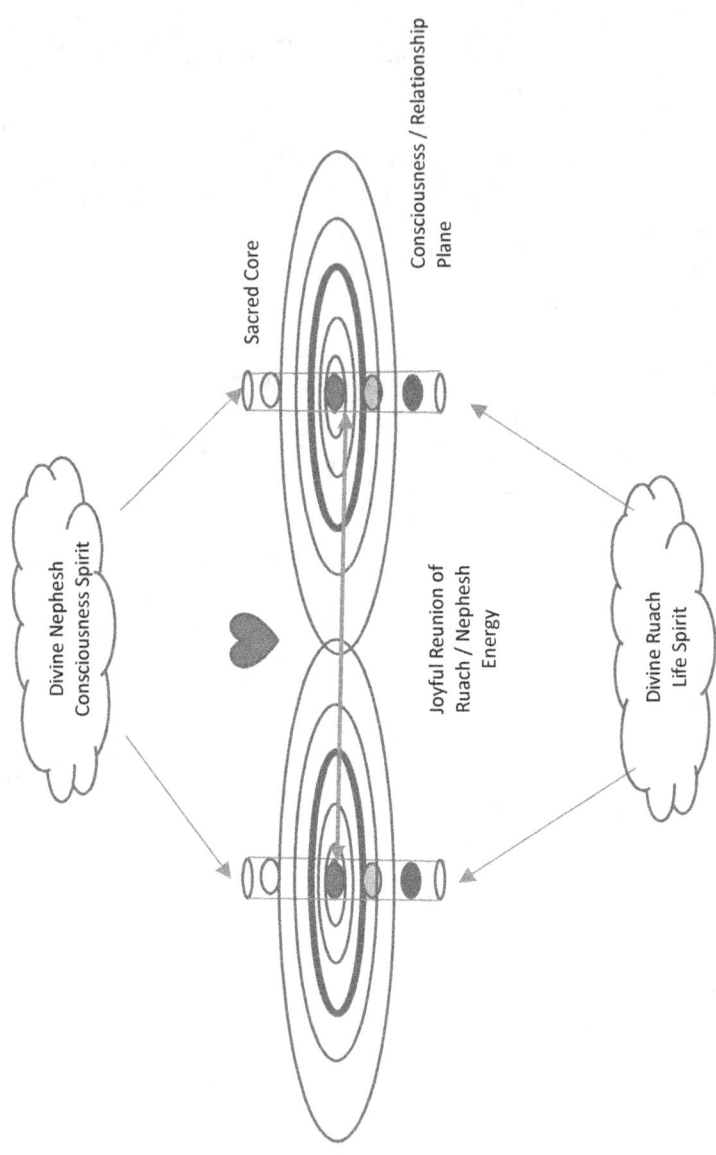

Figure 14: Divine Namaste

Just as Divine Other in Communion with Divine Self radiates into the relationship plane, Divine Other also reaches out through others. The result is Ruach/Nephesh Spiritual Energy reaching into space-time through self and finding joyful reunion with Ruach/Nephesh Spiritual Energy radiating from others.

One may imagine that Divine Other uses the relationship plane to seek out the presence of Divine Other throughout the universe. Every unique manifestation of creativity and love represents Divine Other, reaching into the physical universe to further the causes of increasing conscious creativity and sharing love.

Namaste is a Hindu term that means allowing the Divinity within self to recognize and accept the Divinity within others. In this practice, Divine Namaste is explored. All the previous practices lead to this. Releasing challenges, developing self-awareness and compassion for self, and developing compassion for others contribute to this pursuit. In Namaste meditation, the goal is to allow Divine Other in communion with Sacred Core Self to connect with and celebrate reconciliation with Divine Other emanating from others.

Practice: Divine Namaste

As with all practices, begin with deep breathing. Allow yourself to focus on your diaphragm, rising and falling. With every breath, recognize and release distractions from the environment around you. Move your attention to releasing bodily distractions, and finally to releasing internal thoughts and feelings.

Once stabilized, move your attention to conscious thoughts. Visualize the outermost ring of the consciousness plane and, with a single breath, release. Allow your attention to move to subconscious egos. Smile as you recognize them, each awaiting a situation where they can become active, and with a single breath, release them. Allow your attention to move to the instinct layer where protective identities reside. Smile with appreciation and, with a single breath, release them as well.

Step into your sacred core and recognize the energy flowing along its vertical axis. You are aligned with the Universe and with your Higher Power. You are within your sacred center. Recognize your mind chakra and consciously release any confusion you may be experiencing. Move your attention to your heart chakra and, with a single breath, release attachments. Moving to your core chakra, release fears and doubts. Finally, moving down to your root chakra, recognize any obsessions or guilt that are a part of your life and consciously release them.

Completely free of all distractions, take a moment to breathe. Turn your attention outside your body and simply recognize the beauty, the energy, and the life that exists outside yourself. Breathe and be present.

If you have physical or emotional pain in your life, you may take a moment to visualize the areas where the pain is located and with every breath, release.

When you are satisfied and at peace, take a moment to visualize your Higher Power. With a single breath, invite your Higher Power into your mind chakra and, with gratitude, recognize the clarity and freedom that are available. With another breath, invite your Higher Power into your heart chakra. Again, with gratitude, accept the love that is available. Moving to your core chakra, accept the peace, faith and wisdom that are available. And finally, moving to the root chakra, recognize the joy and passion that is available there.

Breathe and feel Divine Breath Energy rising from the earth like a living flame that warms your root chakra. As Sacred Core rises in communion with Divine Other, recognize your root chakra warming, boiling, and igniting with joy and enthusiasm. With another breath, recognize the core chakra heating, boiling, and igniting with faith and strength. Recognize the heart chakra heating, boiling over, and igniting with love that transcends your physical being. Finally, recognize your mind chakra warming, boiling, and igniting with clarity, hope, and creativity. Sacred Ruach Life energy flows from your root to your mind, and Sacred Nephesh Consciousness Energy flows from your mind to your root. You are alive and glowing with life and consciousness.

Sacred Core energy expands to embrace your instinct level of consciousness. With compassion and gratitude, your protective egos are content. Expanding attention to the subconscious egos, the warmth of compassion provides reassurance. Expanding again to embrace your waking consciousness, sense yourself glowing with joy and peace.

Expanding outside your physical being, recognize your close relationships. Recognize the presence of ego in relationships as well, masking and reflecting authentic connections. Breathe and release any ego-based expectations, and in so doing accept authentic self and others. Allow yourself to be present without any desire to control or

172

change.

Expand your awareness to casual acquaintances through work and life. Breathe and allow yourself to be present. Recognize the Sacred Cores of others, and recognize that they, too, have egos in place for protection and with expectations. Accept them for who they are, where they are. Recognize the ego expectations that you impose, and then release. Allow yourself to be present, without judgment or expectation.

Move your attention out into the unknown. Recognize billions of lives, billions of conscious beings, all with egos, needs, fears, and hopes. Allow your love and compassion to flow. Allow yourself to be present, with your inner light glowing like a beacon of warmth and welcome. Breathe.

Recognize the presence of consciousness within and beyond the physical universe. Recognize the saintly lights that glow with warmth, love, and welcome. With gratitude, allow yourself to connect with the lights. Accept the loving compassion that flows from them to you. Beloved, connected, and belonging, simply breathe and accept.

As you breathe, recognize the connection all beings, all lights, have with Divine Other. Life and Consciousness, Ruach and Nephesh flow in communion with every living creature. Recognize the light that Divine Other provides in the physical universe through these connected beings. Smile and breathe as you simply accept. The universe glows with Divine clarity, love, faith, and joy. Divine Energy radiates and warms all that is touched. Clouded egos may not perceive the light; reflective egos may reject the light; but the light is present. Divine Light never controls, but always invites communion with creativity and love.

As you breathe, recognize Divine Light within yourself, reaching through your Sacred Core and radiating outward. You are glowing with Divine Energy. You exist in communion with Divine Other, radiating love, compassion, and creative consciousness.

Recognize the Divine Energy from within yourself connecting and resonating with Divine Energy from others. Recognize the joyful reunion that takes place within this physical universe, as Divine Energy recognizes and embraces Divine Energy. The reunion of Divine Other with Divine Other is like a celebration feast, a joyous wedding, a celebration of life and consciousness.

And then, breathing, allow yourself to relax. Recognize also the presence of companionable silence. Within the sound of your breath recognize the sense of peace, the presence of Grace. Realize that while there is still suffering and loss in the physical universe, there is also light. Grace abides, present and inviting, glowing from within you, within all living creatures, and throughout the universe. Like a healing balm, Grace abides, offering comfort and reassurance.

With gratitude and compassion, allow yourself to feel positive regard toward yourself. Consider the living souls nearby within your home and surroundings, and allow positive regard to extend to them. Expand your attention to include your local area, including plants, animals, and aquatic life swimming in creeks and waters.

Expand your attention to your local state or province, and further to your country of residence. Breathe and allow your positive regard to flow to human beings and living creatures. Allow your attention to envelope the entire planet Earth. Allow positive regard to flow throughout.

Breathe, smile, and return your attention to self. With peace and love, emerge from your meditation. Allow this experience to provide joy and motivation. Allow your life to be filled with love and creative consciousness. Share your gifts with others. Enjoy the benefits your gifts provide and enjoy the benefits of the gifts that others provide. Use your gifts to be present, to lift up those who are receptive, and to be a reassuring presence. Enjoy life.

As the sun rises, a deer wanders near a stream, a young fawn by her side. She tastes the sweet morning dew as she nibbles the grass. She feels contentment as her fawn nurses. She inhales the cool air and sees her breath as she exhales. She is alive; she is conscious; and she shares companionship and love. There are dangers; there has been and there will be suffering and loss, but here and now, there is presence and Grace. In this moment, here and now is all that matters.

Namaste

REFERENCES

Andorfer, G. & McCain, R. (Producers) (1980, September 28) Cosmos: A Personal Voyage Episode 1: The Shores of the Cosmic Ocean [Television Broadcast]. PBS

Baum, L. F. (1939). The wizard of Oz. Hollywood, Calif.: Metro Goldwyn Mayer.

The Bhagavad-Gita (2022, August 28th) https://bhagavad-gita.org

Buber, Martin (1923/1996) I and Thou. New York, NY: Touchstone

Burke, Peter and Stets, Jan (2009) Identity Theory. Oxford, NY: Oxford University Press.

Buswell, Robert E Jr., Lopez, Donald S. Jr. (2013). The Princeton Dictionary of Buddhism. Princeton University Press. pp. 546, 59, 68.

Cameron, Julia (2016) The Artist's Way: A Spiritual Path to Higher Creativity 25th Anniversary Edition. New York, NY: Penguin Random House LLC

Cassidy J, Jones JD, Shaver PR. Contributions of attachment theory and research: a framework for future research, translation, and policy. Developmental Psychopathology 2013 Nov;25(4 Pt 2):1415-34.

Dodd, M.S., Papineau, D., Grenne, T. et al (2017). Evidence for early life in Earth's oldest hydrothermal vent precipitates. Nature 543(7643) 60-64.

Fehmi, Les and Robbins, Jim (2007) Dissolving Pain: The Open Focus Brain: Harnessing the Power of Attention to Heal Mind and Body. Boston, Ma.: Trumpeter Books

Foster, Richard J. (1992) Prayer: Finding the Heart's True Home. New York, NY.: Harper Collins

Frank, Anne, 1929-1945 author. (1995). The diary of a young girl: the definitive edition. New York : Doubleday

Frankl, V. (Lasch, I. Translator) (1946 / 2006) Man's Search for Meaning. Boston, Ma: Beacon Press

Freud, S. (1923/1964) The Ego and the Id / The standard edition of the complete psychological works of Sigmund Freud (J.Strachey, Ed) London, UK: Macmillon

Kubler-Ross, Elizabeth (1969 / 2014) On Death and Dying. New York, NY: Scribner

Kubler-Ross, Elizabeth (1991 / 2008) On Life After Death. New York, NY: Celestial Arts

Harvey, Peter (Brian Peter). (1990). An introduction to Buddhism: teachings, history, and practices. Cambridge; New York: Cambridge University Press,

Hanson, R., & Mendius, R. (2009). Buddha's brain: The practical neuroscience of happiness, love & wisdom. Oakland, CA: New Harbinger Publications.

Lind, R. E. (2001). Historical Origins of the Modern Mind/Body Split. The Journal of Mind and Behavior, 22(1), 23–40.

Long, Jeffery D. (2013). Jainism: An Introduction. London, UK: I.B. Tauris

Lopez A, Sanderman R., Ranchor, A., Schroevers, M. (2018) Compassion for Others and Self-Compassion: Levels, Correlates, and Relationship with Psychological Well-being. Mindfulness, 9:325-331.

Maslow, A. H. (1943). A theory of human motivation. Psychological Review, 50(4), 370–396.

Nietzsche, F. W., & Kaufmann, W. (1883 / 1995). Thus spoke Zarathustra: A book for all and none. New York: Modern Library.

New Revised Standard Version Bible (1989) London, UK: Harper Collins

The Noble Quran (1975) (Taqi-ud-Din Al-Hilali M. and Muhsin Khan M. Translators) Madinha, KSA: King Fahd Complex for the Printing of the Holy Quran.

Padmakara Translation Group (1997) The way of the Bodhisattva. Boston, Ma: Shambala

Rogers, Fred. (Herman, Karen Interviewer) (1999) Fred Rogers Interview Chapter 7 [Video] Television Academy. https://interviews.televisionacademy.com/interviews/fred-rogers?clip=112589#interview-clips

Schwartz, Richard C. (2001) Introduction to the Internal Family Systems Model Oak Park, Il: Trailheads Publications

Spielberg, Steven, Benchley, Peter. (Producer and Author) (1975) JAWS . USA.

Tanakh. (1985) Philadelphia, Pa.: Jewish Publication Society

Uvnäs-Moberg K, Handlin L, Petersson M. Self-soothing behaviors with particular reference to oxytocin release induced by non-noxious sensory stimulation. Front Psychol. 2015 Jan 12;5:1529.

Warren, Rick (2002) The Purpose Driven Life: What on Earth am I here for? Grand Rapids Mi: Zondervan

Wilber, Ken (2016) Integral Meditation: Mindfulness as a way to grow up, wake up, and show up in your life. Boulder Co: Shambala Publications Inc.

World Bank Group (2022, August 25). Death Rate, Crude (per 1000 people) https://data.worldbank.org/indicator/SP.DYN.CDRT.IN

Yeshe, Thubton, Lama (2001) Introduction to Tantra: The Transformation of Desire. Somerville, Ma.: Wisdom Publications

ABOUT THE AUTHOR

Dave Miller is a retired Professional Counselor and Electronics Engineer with Masters degrees in Theological Studies (Emory University) and Community Counseling (Argosy University Atlanta), and a BS in Electrical Engineering (Milwaukee School of Engineering). Dave has experience in addiction and mental health counseling, Spiritual Direction and Discernment, and Lay Ministry within various churches, agencies, and in private practice. Dave practices, teaches, and has done extensive research in Tantric Buddhist meditation techniques. His first book "Christian Tantric Meditation Guide" was published in 2014.

www.ingramcontent.com/pod-product-compliance
Lightning Source LLC
Chambersburg PA
CBHW071236130626
46556CB00003B/1042